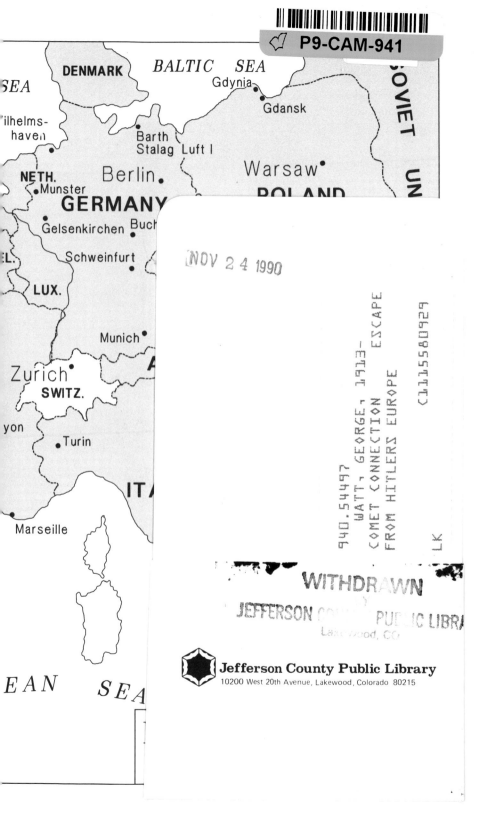

The Comet Connection

The Comet Connection

ESCAPE FROM HITLER'S EUROPE

George Watt

THE UNIVERSITY PRESS OF KENTUCKY

Copyright © 1990 by George Watt

The University Press of Kentucky
Scholarly publisher for the Commonwealth,
serving Bellarmine College, Berea College, Centre
College of Kentucky, Eastern Kentucky University,
The Filson Club, Georgetown College, Kentucky
Historical Society, Kentucky State University,
Morehead State University, Murray State University
Northern Kentucky University, Transylvania University,
University of Kentucky, University of Louisville,
and Western Kentucky University.

Editorial and Sales Offices: Lexington, Kentucky 40506-0336

Library of Congress Cataloging-in-Publication Data

Watt, George, 1913-
    The comet connection : escape from Hitler's Europe / George Watt.
        p.   cm.
    ISBN 0-8131-1720-8 :
    1. Watt, George, 1913-   . 2. World War, 1939-1945—Aerial
operations, American.   3. World War, 1939-1945—Personal narratives,
American.   4. World War, 1939-1945—Underground movements—Belgium.
5. Escapes—Belgium.   6. Flight engineers—United States—Biography.
7. United States.   Army Air Forces—Biography.   I. Title.
D790.W374   1990
940.54'5973'092—dc20   89-70733

For Margie

Contents

[Illustrations follow page 30]

Maps and Figure

My Thanks

To John Taylor and Frederick Pernell of the National Archives in Washington, D.C., and to Victor Berch of the Abraham Lincoln Brigade Archives (ALBA) at Brandeis University.

To Joseph Clark, Ruth Clark, Alan Dawley, Joseph Greene, Betsy Jameson, Jill Jarnow, David Lenfest, Abe Osheroff, Leland Smith, Randall Smith, and Nancy Wechsler, who helped in various ways.

To Ingrid Segers, who acted as interpreter, and to Monique Inghels, who interpreted and opened so many doors in Hamme and Zele.

To Daniel and Molly Watt, who traveled to Belgium to photograph and help with the interviews.

To Steven Watt, who gave encouragement and advice, and to Joseph Watt, my grandson, who at age thirteen said, "It's a good story Grandpa, but it needs editing."

To William Susman, a fellow veteran of the Abraham Lincoln Brigade and World War II, who did just that —spending countless hours with me and my manuscript, destiltifying language, pruning sentences, and offering invaluable suggestions.

And above all, to the one I cannot thank enough, my wife Margie, who was part of the events and part of its telling, and whose love sustained me all the way.

To my family and friends who urged me on, my thanks.

Prologue

In 1984 my wife and I traveled to Belgium in an effort to tie up some loose ends in the story I was writing about my experience in Nazi-occupied Europe. My Belgian friends and I had been out of touch since the end of World War II, and it was a bittersweet reunion. As we came away my wife said, "This book has to be their story too! You owe it to them."

Four days later, in beautiful Nice, a thief broke into the trunk of our rented car and made off with my camera, my tape recorder, 200 shots of undeveloped film, 60 pages of notes, and—to my absolute horror!—six hours of taped interviews.

I had to go back! In the course of preparing my return in 1985, I learned for the first time that the organization that had engineered my escape was the Comet Line. The Line was one of several escape networks operating in Belgium and France. It had saved more people and lasted longer than any other rescue organization. The Gestapo destroyed it several times, but it always reemerged to continue its dangerous mission. It paid a terrible price; for every airman saved, there were two Comet arrests. Many were executed and many died in concentration camps

A twenty-four-year-old Belgian nurse, Andrée de Jongh, was its founder. After Dunkirk, Andrée, with the help of her father, Frédéric, developed a rescue operation for British soldiers stranded in Belgium. Later, using the same network, Dédée, as she became known in the underground, established an escape route from Belgium through France and over the Pyrenees into

Spain. She named it the Comet Line to denote the speed with which airmen were returned to England. Dédée herself had made at least eighteen round trips delivering airmen across the Pyrenees before she was arrested in January 1943. Her indomitable will inspired her coworkers, a majority of whom were women, to acts of extraordinary courage. And women continued to hold leadership positions to the very end.

This book is my tribute to the intrepid women and men of the Comet Line and to the townspeople of Zele and Hamme in Belgium, who risked their lives to protect me.

This book is also an appreciation of my crew. From April 1943, when our B-17 bomber crew was assembled at Pyote Air Base in Texas, till our final mission over Germany seven months later, we were never apart. We went through some rough air battles at Münster, Wihelmshaven, Schweinfurt, Gdynia. We became seasoned veterans, growing attached to one another in the process.

Lt. William Bramwell, a twenty-six-year-old Californian, raised on a Kansas wheat farm, was our commander. Low key, rugged, and competent, his calm efficiency pulled us through some pretty tight scrapes. I still remember returning from the Schweinfurt raid, our plane badly damaged, without enough gas to reach our base. Bramwell flew us through the dangerous London balloon barrage—blimps with chains dangling to keep the Luftwaffe out—and brought us down with a beautiful three-point landing on the short uphill runway of an RAF Spitfire base.

Lt. William (Jim) Current, only nineteen, from New Jersey, our copilot and second in command, was always enthusiastic. Trained as an airplane mechanic before he became a pilot, he knew his ship. I was constantly amazed that one so young could handle such a complex job.

Lt. John Maiorca, twenty-five, from Connecticut, a good-looking man with dark hair, self-assured, warm, and outgoing, was our bombardier and handled one of the nose guns.

Lt. Leland (Smitty) Smith, twenty-two, from the University of Kentucky, was an inquisitive intellectual, always questioning me about the Spanish war. He was a crackerjack navigator and manned the other nose gun.

T/Sgt. H.C. (Tennessee) Johnson, a twenty-year-old carpenter's helper from Bemis, Tennessee, was the flight engineer. He stood in the cockpit monitoring the power instruments and fuel consumption, and operated the top turret. I liked H.C., and we were good friends, even though I thought I should have been the engineer because I was ten years older and more mature. But we had tossed a coin for the position, and he won.

Our conscientious radio operator, T/Sgt. Albertus Harrenstein, twenty-six, from Iowa, was high strung and excitable. I used to think those traits were requirements for radio operators. He manned a gun through the top window of the radio room.

S/Sgt. Joseph Sage, twenty-five, a native of the Bronx, a New York University graduate, and a former metropolitan golf champion, was our ball turret operator.

S/Sgt. Leslie Meader, twenty-three, from Minnesota, had a pleasant manner and a quiet sense of humor. He was assistant radio operator and left waist gunner.

S/Sgt. John Craig, nineteen, a likable kid from California, handled the tail guns.

I, a staff sergeant and New Yorker, pushing thirty—oldest man on the crew—was assistant flight engineer and right waist gunner.

The volunteers of the Abraham Lincoln Brigade, with whom I served in the Spanish Civil War from 1937 to 1939, are also part of this story. They were the first Americans to take up arms against Hitler and Mussolini, who were supporting Franco. That war was the opening battle against Hitlerism and a dress rehearsal for World War II. Instead of welcoming our combat experience, we were considered "premature anti-Fascists" and initially kept from going overseas. But a change in War Department policy in the spring of 1943 permitted Lincoln Brigade veterans to go into combat, making it possible for me to join the Bramwell crew.

This is the memoir of one American's second chance at Hitler. The participants were many. I salute them all.

PART I. Walking Out

1

Happy Birthday at Happy Valley

November 5, 1943, Knettishall, England.

"Bramwell's Crew! Grab your socks!"

I was startled out of a deep sleep. My watch said six o'clock—but there'd been no alert the night before, and they usually woke us between one and two-thirty when we were scheduled to fly.

Suddenly, I remembered that it was my thirtieth birthday—one day I did not want to fly.

The night before, some of us had been sitting around the stove in our Quonset hut chewing the fat. "Tomorrow is my birthday," I said. "I've always said if I live to thirty, I'll live to a ripe old age. I have to confess," I added, "five years ago in Spain I was saying, 'If I live to twenty-five, I'll live to a ripe old age.'"

"What were you doing in Spain?" Grundlach, a replacement gunner, piped up.

"I fought in the Spanish Civil War."

"Come on! You're old, but not that old."

"The Spanish *Civil* War, not the Spanish *American* War." I knew that was coming. I'd heard it before.

"What the hell were you doing there? Were you a soldier of fortune or somethin'?"

"You kidding? At 100 pesetas a month? You couldn't buy Mexican chickpeas with that. No, I was a soldier of freedom." It sounded pat, and I was immediately sorry I'd said it. "Actually it was the beginning of this war. We were fighting the same enemies, Hitler and Mussolini. They helped Franco overthrow the Spanish Republican government. I thought that if we stopped them there we might prevent this one."

"But why you? Why did *you* have to go?"

"I felt strongly about that son of a bitch Hitler and his concentration camps. I hated his master race crap. I felt I had to go. About 3,000 Americans felt the same way."

The guys had gone on to kid me about my flexible superstition but—in deference to my advanced age, I suppose—assured me that I had made it. There would be no mission the next day; the fog was too thick. And it certainly looked that way from the weather reports we'd been getting all night. You never saw a bunch more sensitive to weather than these guys in my squadron. As each new airman came in from the movies or Aero club, we got a full report on clouds, stars, and moon. We asked if an alert was on. Did they load bombs? How many? How much gas in the tanks?

Their answers constituted our "barracks briefing." Thousand-pounders meant docks or submarine pens. Five-hundred-pounders and incendiaries meant factories or rail centers. Full "Tokyo" (auxiliary belly) tanks threatened DPs (deep penetrations) into western or central Germany. Clear weather meant France or Belgium; 10/10th overcast (maximum cloud cover) spelled Germany.

Now, as I was getting dressed, I still didn't think we'd fly that morning. The fog had closed in thicker than ever, and I was sure the mission would be scrubbed. "Well, fellas," I said cheerfully, "I've reached my thirtieth, all right."

"Wait," Oscar Land said. "The day ain't over yet." Reluctantly, I had to admit he was right.

"Okay. We'll celebrate at the club tonight."

The atmosphere was tense as we got to the briefing room. To tell the truth, it was always tense. But that particular morning, perhaps because it was my birthday, I was more uptight than usual. The enlisted men, wearing flight jackets with brightly painted names—"Joho's Jokers," "Screamin' Red Ass," "Cock o' the Walk," "Princess Pat," "Little Boy Blue"—were already seated and chattering noisily. We noncoms were always briefed before the officers.

Hidden behind a large screen, waiting for the "unveiling," was the dreaded map that would show us the flight route to and from the target, with the concentrations of enemy flak marked by red cellophane overlay. Everyone was speculating about where we were going. When we were all seated, the bright young A2 (Air Intelligence) officer raised the screen.

We sat there in stunned silence, our eyes following the black ribbon to the solid red mass surrounding the target. There was a soft whistle. Someone said, "Uh, uh!" That broke the spell. Now everyone was talking at once.

We were going to "Happy Valley"! We'd been expecting a mission to the Ruhr Valley for some time. But dammit, why did it have to be on my birthday?

It took some quieting down by the A2 officer before he was able to start the briefing. "Men, your target today is Gelsenkirchen, one of the most important rail centers in the Ruhr. You will leave the coast of England at this point." He spoke in a cold, emotionless tone as he used a long pointer to trace our route. "One group of P-47s will meet you here and take you to the IP (Initial Point, the last turn before the bomb run). Another group of P-47s will join you at the IP and take you past the target. You will have escort all the way to the target area and all the way back to the coast of Belgium."

Escort all the way in! At least that was a consolation, and the first time we'd had it for a DP. I still shudder when I think of the Schweinfurt raid. Our fighters took us a little way past the English Channel and left us. As we approached the IP, we saw scores of parachutes floating in the air. These were our men whose planes had already gone down. It looked more like a parachute jump than an air raid. Then swarms of German fighters attacked us in force. Without any fighter escort, we caught hell. Sixty planes and six hundred men were lost that day. President Roosevelt said our country could not afford such losses.

Now, for the first time, our fighters were equipped with auxiliary belly tanks that could be jettisoned when they were emptied. This gave the fighters enough fuel to escort us all the way to the target and back.

"As you see by the route," the briefing officer continued in the same tone, "you will encounter very little flak, except when you come to the Ruhr Valley. Here, of course, men, you will meet heavy antiaircraft fire from their 88s and 105s. You can also expect to be attacked by heavy concentrations of Focke-Wulf 190s and Messerschmidt 109s. There will be the usual diversionary attacks by medium bombers in order to draw off the enemy fighters.

"You will now see a photo of the target. Lights out, please. Here you see the target, the railroad marshaling yards. You will approach the target at a heading of 180 degrees. That is all. Any questions? Good luck."

We filed out, our faces grim. Waiting outside for the second briefing shift, the officers—pilots, navigators, and bombardiers—anxiously scanned our faces for clues to the nature of the mission. We were not permitted to talk to them. Breaking the rule, someone said, "This is no milk run!"

We had about two hours till takeoff. That gave us plenty of time to collect our flying togs, place our guns in the ship, check them out, and bullshit with the ground crew.

I went down to the drying room to draw my electric-heated suit, then to the parachute shop for my chute pack. I picked up stuff from my locker, packed the whole load on my bicycle, and lumbered like a fully loaded bomber to the dispersal area where our B-17 Flying Fortress was waiting. She was battle scarred with hundreds of flak holes, but she'd always brought us back. After each mission we counted the holes and counted our blessings as we went to debriefing.

I feel sorry to this day that we never got to paint her name on the fuselage. Long after the crew or ship is gone the name lives on. After a lot of haggling, we had finally chosen the name *Butcher Boy*. I didn't particularly like it but was willing to settle for it. The idea was Sage's. We had planned to have it painted on that very day, if we didn't fly. The Butcher Boy was to be Porky, of Walt Disney fame, carrying a paper bag filled with sausages. The bag would be torn at one end, and as each sausage dropped out of the bag, it would turn into a bomb. Each bomb would then become the symbol for a mission completed.

Gun positions also had names. Some I still remember: "Pete and Repete," "Big Dick," "Shoot, You're Faded." Sage, the other homesick New Yorker in our crew, named his ball turret guns "42nd Street" and "Times Square." I had wanted to call my waist gun "Doran's Revenge" for Dave Doran, a friend who was killed in Spain, but I decided it was too somber. So it became —what else?—"Watt's Cookin'."

I was all set, with my gun and equipment in place, when I suddenly remembered I had a $50 money order in my wallet that should be sent home to my wife, Margie. I hopped on my bike, pedaled frantically back to the barracks, penned a short note, then rushed back to our pilot, Lieutenant Bramwell, to have it censored, and I still had twenty minutes to spare. What a relief that I'd remembered in time!

We exchanged the ritual ribbing with the ground crew—our way of covering up how much we depended on those guys and how much they worried about our coming back—then boarded our ship and got ready for takeoff.

Meader, Sage, and I always got into our flying togs while the ship taxied down the apron to takeoff position. It was quite a procedure. First, we took off our boots and stripped down to our long johns. Next, we donned electric-heated suits and electric-heated boots. Over the heated suit went a summer flying suit, and over the heated boots a pair of heavy fleece-lined flying boots. Then we put on a winter flying helmet with built-in earphones, snap-on oxygen mask, and connecting hose, and over the helmet we wore flying goggles. We had three pairs of gloves—silk next to the skin, electrically heated gloves over the silk, and, aloft, a pair of heavy RAF fleece-lined mittens over the other two. Temperatures got to 55 below zero with the winds rushing up to 200 miles an hour through our open waist gun positions.

Then came a "Mae West" inflatable life vest, and over that a parachute harness (the chute itself would be snapped on only if we had to use it). Later, over enemy territory, we would add an armored flak suit that weighed a ton, plus a steel infantry helmet. We were plugged into our gun positions by electric wire, interphone lines, and oxygen tubes. We would begin breathing oxygen at 10,000 feet in order to minimize the effects of the bends.

One important item that I forgot to take from my locker that day was an army issue .45 pistol with holster, belt, and two extra clips of ammunition.

We barely managed to complete all these preparations by the time Bramwell turned our Fort into takeoff position. The lead plane was just airborne as the second was lumbering down the middle and our own ship began rolling. Three fully loaded bombers on that one runway, just thirty seconds apart. How we sweated those takeoffs!

Soon we were aloft. What we did not know, as our giant Fortress flew blind through a heavy overcast, was that this was to be our longest misson.

2

Here Comes the Flak

It was one of those drab autumn days you find so often in England. The sky was gray. The 10/10ths layer of clouds above us had to be scaled before we could rendezvous with our group.

When we finally came through the clouds, we saw hundreds of B-17s rattailing all over the sky. Gradually the formations began to take shape, but our own twenty-one-plane group was nowhere in sight. We were still chasing after the big "H" on the tail and looking for the signal flares identifying our 388th Bomb Group when we made a disturbing discovery. Our ball turret was out of commission!

It had checked out okay on the ground. But now Sage, the ball turret gunner, could not disengage the electric clutch that allowed the turret to swing around from the stowed position.

We were frantic. We tried everything. We coaxed it gently. We pleaded with it. We kicked it, shook it, cursed it. Still it wouldn't give. While one man worked on the turret, the others kept providing refilled walk-around oxygen bottles. We were above 25,000 feet, where you cannot live more than a few minutes without oxygen. Every ounce of energy expended saps all your strength. We worked over that turret for at least an hour—to no avail.

We finally caught up with our group at 29,000 feet, just as it was beginning to head out across the Channel. Bramwell consulted the crew on whether to abort or go on. This was our seventh mission. The magic number was twenty-five; after that we could go home. Bramwell decided not to abort.

Sage sat down to sweat out the mission without his guns. We all sweated with him. The ball turret with its twin 50-caliber machine guns was not just another position. It commanded the entire hemisphere below.

I used to watch Joe Sage squeeze his stocky 5'11" frame into that ball, where he would sit cramped in a fetal position for hours on end. He was encapsulated from the rest of the plane with nothing but plexiglass between him and the ground. Just thinking about it used to give me the willies. But Sage, a former golf champion, approached his task with the same meticulous care and control that he applied to sinking a putt.

We headed out over the North Sea, following a circuitous route designed to confuse the enemy and crossing onto the Continent at the Zuyder Zee in Holland.

Vapor trails began to appear at three o'clock high. Soon the sky was covered with these white contrails as far as the eye could see. How we loved that sight! The streamers were made by P-47 Thunderbolts, our fighter escort. Some were 5,000 feet above us. Others, falling into position alongside us, hugged us closely. Still others were far off to the side, sallying forth to seek out enemy fighters.

I put on my heavy flak suit and steel infantry helmet. Flak, so far, was not too bad. Over the beach we hit the usual coastal defenses—inaccurate bursts, not very heavy. We were soon through them.

For the next half-hour we flew in relative security along the flak-free highway plotted for us by A2. I had too much time to think about the battle ahead. I looked across the waist at Meader and at Sage, who was sitting outside the radio room. With oxygen masks covering their faces, I could see only their eyes peering anxiously through their goggles.

We hit the IP, made a sharp turn, headed due south for Gelsenkirchen—and the action started. Our bomb bay doors were already open when enemy fighters appeared. They were not yet in sufficient force to break through to our formations; they were being engaged by our own fighters. We couldn't take our eyes off the dogfights, but we kept an alert eye on the skies around us for any enemy planes that might penetrate our defenses.

Maiorca announced Gelsenkirchen up ahead. Then, his voice rising, he shouted, "There's the flak!"

He didn't have to tell us. All hell broke loose. Big black bursts of smoke flowered all around us. The flak was so thick you could walk on it. We could barely see the other ships in our formation. Our giant Fort rocked and shook like a cork on a rough sea. We heard the clash of metal against metal as the flak ripped into our plane. Our ears were bursting from the concussion.

Over the interphone came copilot Current's excited voice: "Number One engine is hit! Looks like it's on fire. Will someone check it out?"

There was no answer.

Current pleaded again, "Is Number One on fire? Will someone tell me?"

I looked away from my own position across to the left waist and called back, "Oil gushing out. Thick black smoke. No flame showing. But it's burning, all right."

Suddenly I felt yanked toward the ceiling as the plane sideslipped out of formation, dropping 2,000 feet.

"Pilot to crew. Prepare to bail out," came Bramwell's remarkably calm voice. We tore off our flak suits and hooked on our chest packs. But under Bramwell's quick and skillful handling of the ship, the smoke gradually disappeared. Lucky for us it was just an oil and not a gasoline fire. Still, the loss of oil made it impossible to feather the prop (that is, streamline the propeller into the wind so that it doesn't spin). We could not get enough power from the other three engines to get back into the formation against the drag of the windmilling prop.

We were still with the group when Maiorca saw a town below

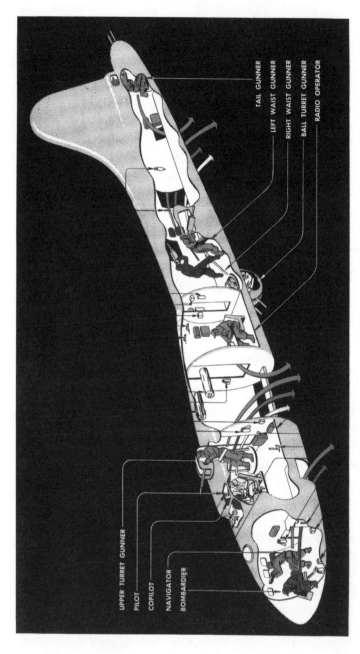

UPPER TURRET GUNNER
PILOT
COPILOT
NAVIGATOR
BOMBARDIER

TAIL GUNNER
LEFT WAIST GUNNER
RIGHT WAIST GUNNER
BALL TURRET GUNNER
RADIO OPERATOR

B-17F Crew Positions and Emergency Exits

and said he was dropping his bombs. But flying "tail-end Charley," dragging along behind and below the others, made us a sitting duck. So Bramwell banked the ship to the right, and Current announced, "We're heading back. We're on our own, boys. Keep your eyes peeled for fighters." We unhooked our chest packs and settled back into our gun positions again.

Current shot up a distress signal. Four Thunderbolts quickly swooped down on us. As they hugged us closely, cavorting playfully about us, weaving and crisscrossing back and forth, we felt secure.

When it was time for our ten-minute oxygen check, Current called over the interphone, "Copilot to crew. Oxygen check."

The answers came back:

"Top turret, okay."

"Right waist, okay."

"Left waist, okay."

"Radio, okay."

"Sage, okay."

"Bombardier, okay."

No response from the navigator. No response from the tail gunner. I didn't know then that Smitty's oxygen system had failed and that Maiorca's quick thinking saved his life. I was looking back to the tail, where all I could see was the soles of Craig's feet, his toes pointed down. Sage came over and hooked up to my waist gun, while I grabbed my chute pack and a walk-around oxygen bottle and crawled the thirty feet back to the tail.

I found Craig lying face down, unconscious, his color a deep deathly blue. His oxygen mask was drawn down below his nose. I pulled it back up and turned on the emergency valve for pure oxygen. My own walk-around bottle was now empty, so I kept switching Craig's mask back and forth between us. His color gradually came back, and he revived. But I was leery of leaving him alone in the tail, so I refilled the walk-around bottle and told

him to go back to the waist where there were others in case he
had trouble again.

I laid my chute behind me and settled down at the tail gun
position.

A few minutes later I spoke to Craig over the interphone. He
was resting comfortably in the radio room. He sounded cheerful
and said he was okay.

When Smitty, our navigator, announced that we were over
Belgium in sight of the coast, cruising at 20,000 feet, we felt as if
we were going to make it. Then one of the P-47s came down
close, wiggled its wings in a farewell salute, and peeled off for
home. We knew they had stayed with our crippled ship as long as
they could, perhaps longer than was safe for them. With their
limited supply of gas, they could not keep up with our slow pace
and hope to get back. A fighter low on gas over enemy territory
is more vulnerable than a crippled bomber. All the guns are in
the nose and wing, and the pilot can fire at his enemy only by
outmaneuvering him. That takes speed and power and requires
extra fuel. But a Fort's guns point in all directions. It can at least
take care of itself in a pinch.

We felt no grudge against the fighters for leaving us. We were
grateful they had brought us that far. But now the feeling of
aloneness crept over me. It must have enveloped every other
member of the crew as well. It was early afternoon; the sun was
shining; the ceiling was unlimited. We could see the ground, and
the ground could see us. I felt as conspicuous as a man walking
naked across Times Square.

Our escort had hardly left us when I spotted a black speck of a
plane coming up at five o'clock low. I called him out. He was
way out of range. He began swinging around to our left. I called
again, "It's a Focke-Wulf 190. Low, moving toward seven
o'clock. Watch him, Johnson."

"I got him," said H.C. from his top turret.

He was at nine o'clock now, still out of range, getting ready to attack us from the left. No need to waste ammunition. Wait till he commits himself to the attack.

"Here he comes! Johnson! Meader! He's all yours. Let him have it!"

I could only sit and sweat him out till he swooped around to the tail. Most lateral attacks develop into tail attacks. The fighter, as he closes in, has to point his nose not at you but at some point that will put his shells in the exact spot where you will be a second or less after he has fired. In order to compensate for his rate of closure, he must constantly change his angle until he is pointed in the same direction as your ship. This brings him around behind your tail. It is at the end of this maneuver, called the "pursuit curve," that your assailant presents the best target to the tail gunner. Of course, when you divorce the mathematics of this fascinating little game from the reality, you realize that you also make a better target to him.

I realized that soon enough. I could see him blinking at us, and an instant later I heard his 20mm shells exploding in our plane. Our tracers were not hitting him. They were going a little too high. How we needed those ball turret guns now! That Focke-Wulf must have known that our belly guns were not working. He stayed just low enough to keep our top turret from getting a good shot at him.

He was swinging around becoming larger and larger. Now I could almost locate him in my tail gun sight. I was tense, waiting for the shots that should be the easiest of all: keep him in your gun sight, and you've nailed him. Well, here he was now, the perfect target.

I lined him up. I pushed the trigger.

Nothing happened.

I pulled the charging handle. It was frozen tight. I looked up and saw that ugly Focke-Wulf with guns blazing, bearing down on me like a fast express train. I panicked. I crouched down behind the armor plate. I tried to make myself as small as possible.

It was not the first time I had known such fear. In my first action at Fuentes del Ebro in Spain, six years earlier, we had been dive-bombed by German Stukas. I lay shivering with fright in a shallow communications trench as the near misses exploded all around us. Now I felt that same kind of terror again.

The panic lasted only a moment. The next instant I felt shame and looked up. He was still bearing down on me. I tried to unjam the guns.

Too late! The next thing I knew, the giant Fort was standing on her nose.

3

No Regrets, No Regrets

It took me a few seconds to realize we were going down. So this was it! The dreaded moment for every flyer.

I tried the interphone. It was dead. I turned around for my chest pack. It wasn't there! When the ship nosed over, everything loose slid down to the waist.

What a careless fool! Flying my usual position at the waist, I had always thought of every last detail in preparation for possible disaster. I wedged my chute in so it couldn't shake loose. Next to my chute I had a pair of strong G.I. boots for "walking out." Now I didn't even have a parachute.

The ship was gathering speed, and the roar was rising to a deafening crescendo. I tried to figure out what had happened. Were the controls shot away? Was the pilot hit? Perhaps both? We were going down faster and faster. Where the hell was my chute? I was beginning to lose all hope of getting out alive. Out of touch with the others, I was damned lonely in the tail. I had to do something. I slid down into the waist.

Once I got there, I couldn't move. The pressure pinned me to the floor. Now I completely gave up. I kept waiting for the crash, kept seeing myself blown to smithereens.

So this was how men died in planes. People have asked me whether it's true that your whole life flashes before your eyes, and at the risk of sounding corny, I must say that mine did. As the ship continued down, a calm enveloped me. The fear was gone. I don't say this to sound heroic. I've learned in two wars that fear is nothing to be ashamed of.

I had faced death before, but in those situations I had been too busy fighting or running or even too damned scared to think about it. Perhaps the closest I came to the feeling of inescapable death was during the retreats in Spain when the Lincolns were surrounded by the Fascists and we had to break out of encirclement. Then it wasn't fear so much as a certain resignation—a determination to survive but to go down fighting if we had to.

Now I was going down, but there was no fighting. There was no way out. I thought of Ruth. She had died soon after giving birth to our son, Danny. I thought of Margie, who had helped rebuild a life for me and Danny after Ruth's death. How much I loved her. And Danny, only two and a half when I left for the army. And my parents and my sister Mae. I was feeling terribly sorry for them. They would all miss me. Well, it couldn't be helped, that's all. Just couldn't be helped.

Suddenly I remembered my birthday. What a cruel irony. How dramatic. How fitting that I should end my life with a nice round number like thirty. I had tempted the fates by joking about it— the guys in the squadron would remember that. Would Margie and Danny know? It wasn't important. But still, I wanted them to know.

It felt like a dream. It wasn't me this was happening to.

The plane was still going down . . . down. When was that ground going to hit?

I felt a little sad at my approaching death, but two words kept running through my mind. No regrets. No regrets. I believe I must have spoken them aloud. No regrets, because I had lived my life the way I wanted it. I knew what comradeship among men and women meant. I knew what it was to love and be loved. I had had my share of personal hardship and deep personal tragedy, but above all I had had that special kind of happiness which comes to one who can say he has lived his life with a purpose. I had volunteered to fight against Fascism in Spain.

And I had volunteered to fly in this war against Hitler. I had no regrets.

A powerful hand still held me glued to the spot. When were we going to hit?

Then something began to happen. The pressure was easing. The plane was leveling off. I could move. Maybe, maybe there was hope.

I was all action now. I ripped the oxygen mask off my face. I struggled to my feet and looked around. Everything was scattered on that waist compartment floor—individual dinghies, flak suits, helmets, ammo cans, ammo belts. Finally, there it was! There was my chute! I snapped it to my harness.

Meader was moving now. And someone else back near the radio room was moving. The ship was still going down but not as fast. There was no time to waste. I had no idea how high we were.

"Let's get the fuck out of here!" I shouted.

Meader had the same idea. We reached the waist door at the same time.

I pulled the emergency cord. Nothing happened. I tried opening the door. It didn't give. I tried to kick it but I was off balance. So while Meader yanked on the emergency release, I threw my shoulder against the door.

The next thing I knew, I was hurtling head over heels through space.

4

"Ici Belgique?"

I don't think I can describe the feelings that raced over me as the prop wash whipped me through that free air. There was unbridled exhilaration, a wild joy at being alive. A moment earlier I'd been dead. Now I was born again. What a wonderful rebirth.

I wondered why I was saved. How come my luck had held out through so many close calls? Suddenly my elation was replaced by concern for the rest of the crew. Where were the others? I looked for the ship. She was above me, still gliding down. I thought I had seen one chute open—which meant eight men were still in that death trap. I shouted and pleaded with them: "Get out of there, you bastards! Come on, bail out!"

I lost sight of the plane and once again became completely concerned with myself. I had stopped spinning. There was no sensation of falling. Everything was so quiet and peaceful. Only someone who has ridden the waist of a B-17 before the days of the pressurized cabin can appreciate how noisy it is, the roar something between a boiler factory and a Seventh Avenue subway. Now the silence was overwhelming. Everything seemed to stop—noise, movement, even time.

I had no way of judging how long I'd been falling. I didn't want to open my chute too soon because free fall speeds your descent, giving you a better chance to get away.

I started to count to ten. By the time I got to eight I was nervous as hell and couldn't hold out. I reached over for the "D" ring on the left side of my chest pack. Where the hell was it? Somewhat panicky, I felt all over the left side. Then a flash of memory—of course, this was a chest pack, not the seat pack we had used in training. The handle was on the right.

I found it and pulled. A short piece of cable came loose in my hand. I looked at it. It should be longer, I thought. Maybe it was shot away? "Dammit! Do I have to go through this dying all over again?" I swear these were my exact words.

Frantically, I reached down to rip open the flap. It was already open. The white umbrella chute was slowly trickling upward. I remembered the scene in *The Great Dictator* when Charlie Chaplin, thinking he is flying right side up, takes a drink from his canteen and the water falls upward.

I was still engrossed in this curiosity when I felt myself yanked up chest first a hundred feet. It felt as if my head and feet had formed a "U" with my back.

Now all movement seemed to stop. I started to look around for the plane and the other chutes. I spotted the ship off in the distance still above me. Three chutes were already open. There went another. And another. Thank God. Just as the seventh chute opened, that old Fort, smoke billowing behind her, dipped her left wing and, swerving gracefully, pointed her nose down for the final plunge.

Suddenly I saw the Focke-Wulf come down, heading straight for the cluster of chutes. The bastards had been known to strafe our boys in the air. I waited horrified and helpless. But he flew on past them and disappeared. I breathed a sigh of relief.

I began to concentrate on my own escape. I could see the ground more clearly now and tried to form a picture of the terrain. The sun was over my left shoulder. In front of me was a winding river. I was falling toward one side of the river; the rest of the crew, some distance away, seemed to be falling toward the other. With my back to the sun I mentally mapped a triangle of three towns: one ahead of me to the left, another on my left but slightly behind me, the largest to my right and forward. I decided to avoid all towns. I looked around for forest to hide in, but could see none. There were only open fields, bordered by trees and what I surmised were hedgerows. And, of course, the river.

I started to rehearse my French, repeating, *"Je suis americain. Je veux me cacher. Je suis americain."*

The ground rushed up at me, interrupting my escape plans. A number of details crowded in. The river was too damn close! I was headed right for it. A church steeple in the distance. A plowed field. A tall stump standing in the field I was about to hit.

I pulled on the shroud lines and looked up from the ground, just as we had been trained to do. I hit hard. My knees buckled and I landed flat on my back, with the wind knocked out of me.

As soon as I caught my breath, I stood up and started to look around. The river was scarcely thirty yards away—too close for comfort. I was in a plowed field bordered by the river on one side, an irrigation ditch lined with shrubbery on another, and a narrow dirt lane on a third. Near the opposite end of the field stood the stump. But it wasn't a stump; it was a man. He stood there motionless, leaning on a hoe. The stony silence, the statuelike stillness of the farmer, and my abrupt thrust into the three-dimensional world on the ground created an odd sense of unreality.

But first things first. I had to hide my chute and gear. I unstrapped my harness and pulled the chute over to the bushes near the river. I removed my helmet and goggles, my heavy flying boots, and my Mae West and tried to push all this stuff together with my bulky chute and harness under the bushes. The chute stubbornly refused to disappear.

I looked at the man. He hadn't moved from the spot. I walked up to him with outstretched hand and said in my carefully rehearsed French, *"Je suis americain. Aviateur. S'il vous plait, je veux me cacher."*

The "stump" was alive after all. With a broad grin that stretched from ear to ear, he shook my hand warmly. I was still a little out of breath, so thinking he might not have heard me, I started again: *"Je suis americain. Je veux me cacher."* Still no response. He just stood there grinning.

I asked if he spoke French. He kept smiling but shook his head.

"Sprechen sie Deutsch"? No dice again.

I was getting desperate. For a minute I thought perhaps I was not in Belgium.

"Ici Belgique?" I asked.

He understood that and nodded his head. Now I remembered. They speak two languages in Belgium, Walloon (French) and Flemish. This fellow spoke only Flemish.

I'll have to find someone who speaks French or German, I thought. But first I must hide, get away from this spot. No telling how soon the Germans will get here.

I had started to say goodbye to the man when from one corner of the field I heard voices. A man and a little girl burst through the bushes and came running toward me. The man shook my hand vigorously and threw one arm around me. I allowed myself to be shaken and tried my French again. This time it worked.

But we had no chance to talk. The quiet of the countryside was abruptly broken by loud voices, dogs barking, bushes rustling. From three sides of the field people were rushing at me. Old men, old women, young kids and dogs, healthy-looking peasant girls with rosy outdoor complexions. They appeared out of nowhere. It looked as if a whole village had come out to greet me. I was reminded of a comedy scene from an old French silent movie.

It's not good to get caught in a crowd, I thought. Stay away from crowds. I must get away. But I couldn't run. I kept desperately edging toward the outskirts of the field, but I had to shake hands with everyone rushing at me.

Concern for my personal safety completely vanished, as I was momentarily transformed from the hunted airman to an ambassador of hope and liberation. I stood there trying to look cool and confident. As each one approached, I rattled off a few words of cheer in French, in German, and in pantomime.

"Death to Hitler! Death to the oppressors! We will win." I said.

"Yes," they said, "but when . . . when . . . when? When will the war be over? When are your soldiers coming to free us? It's taking so long."

I couldn't make any promises. "I don't know when, but there will be an invasion soon. The hour of liberation is not far off." I said again and again, "We will win. We are all united."

But this couldn't go on. I had to return to reality. I must get away at once. I asked them where I could hide. They looked at each other and shrugged their shoulders. I was sorry I had asked. I should have sensed that in a crowd no one would risk an answer.

"Vite, vite," someone shouted, pointing over my shoulder.

I turned around. A man in a black uniform was racing toward me across the field. I wanted to run, but as in a nightmare, my feet just wouldn't move. He was already too close for me to hope to get away over that open stretch. Now I'm done for, I thought.

The crowd drew back as the man came up panting for breath. He started to talk to the villagers in Flemish, seeming to ask them what was going on. I knew now, with some relief, that he wasn't a German after all. He was a Belgian *gendarme*.

It was hard for me to follow what they were saying. One man seemed to be telling the policeman that I was an American *aviateur,* and he should turn me in. Others seemed to be arguing with him. I finally mustered up my courage and spoke to him.

"I am American," I said in my halting French. "America is a friend of the Belgians. We are fighting to liberate Belgium from the Germans. The Americans are coming very soon, and the Germans will be driven out. As a Belgian patriot, you should not turn me over to the Germans." Villagers now seemed to be chiming in on my side.

He stared at me intently as I spoke. His face turned pale and he seemed to be shaken, struggling to make up his mind. Slowly he turned his face to his right, looking across the field to the spot where I had landed. A crowd of people, mostly women, were gathered around my gear, fingering the silk of my parachute. He walked slowly over to them, looking very much like a traffic cop coming upon an accident.

"Vite, vite," the villagers said to me.

"Which way?" I asked. Each one pointed in a different direction, so I just took off toward the dirt lane. A sharp pain pierced my ankle. I must have turned it when I hit the ground.

A few villagers ran after me pointing to my foot, asking, *"Blessé?* Wounded?"

"No," I answered and kept limping along.

People were still rushing into the field. When they saw me, they just took off after me. A beautiful redhead came through the hedgerow and pointed to my new leather flight jacket with my name plate on it. Without losing stride, I took it off and handed it to her.

The crowd was still following on foot and on bicycle. I kept shooing them away. Many of the adults began to drop away, but the kids and dogs still trailed behind. They were like a vapor trail pointing directly to me.

A middle-aged man on a bicycle caught up with me. He was wearing a tweed jacket and cap, a shirt and tie and knicker-bockers. He pointed to a ditch along the dirt road and urged me to get down and hide. But here my class bias came to the fore: to me he looked like a country squire, and I didn't trust him. Besides, the place looked too exposed. I disregarded his advice and kept running.

By now the kids and dogs had gotten the message, however,

and they too stopped following me. I left the lane and crossed into the field on my left. As I did so, I became aware of a man running parallel with me in the field to my left and about two hundred yards ahead. He was wearing a cap. From time to time he motioned for me to continue running. He kept this up for a considerable distance. At last he stopped and pointed to a spot for me to hide. I crouched in my old infantry manner, using every bit of available cover, and made my way to the spot.

Above, Texas, April 1943. Our B-17 crew is assembled. Standing, left to right, are H.C. Johnson, George Watt, Albertus Harrenstein, Leslie Meader, Joseph Sage, and John Craig. Kneeling are William Bramwell, William Current, Leland Smith, and John Maiorca. Below, Lokeren, Belgium, November 5, 1943. The wreckage of our B-17 is strewn among the tombstones in the town cemetery. The Germans had cordoned off the area, but Raoul Steyaert, a fireman and a member of the Belgian Secret Army, managed to take this photo.

Above, Marsa, Catalonia, 1938. Famed photographer Robert Capa captured this poignant moment as the Americans of the Lincoln Battalion were leaving, their fighting days in the Spanish Civil War over. Left to right in front are Capt. Donald Thayer, Maj. Milton Wolff, and Political Commissar George Watt. Left, my International Brigade identity book, carried inside my beret, survived a swim of the Ebro during my escape from Spain.

Right, after swimming the Ebro, I stand with John Gates, right, XVth Brigade Political Commissar, the highest ranking American officer in Spain at the time. Below, more American survivors of the retreats. I'm at left front.

Alois (Weis) Van den Bossche in 1985. From the air, as I was about to make my parachute landing, he looked like a stump.

Omer Van Hecke and his sister Celine, at right, found me in the field and invited me to their home. For forty years I thought they were in the underground. "We just wanted to feed you," they later told me. Rafael, their older sister, is at left.

Mathilde and Eduard Lauwaert still live in this house, my first indoor hideout in Belgium. Left to right, Monique Inghels, Schepen J. de Geyter (a Hamme official), Margie in front of me, Eduard Lauwaert, Yvonne Inghels, and Mathilde Lauwaert almost hidden by her children and grandchildren. Photo courtesy of Marc de Waele.

Left, Eduard stands in the door of the outhouse where I hid while Mathilde put their son Lucien to bed.

Raymond and Yvonne Inghels's wedding photo. Raymond was the irrepressible seaman who took me on the tram to Antwerp and by train to Brussels to the home of Hedwige and Dr. Jean Proost.

Below, Margie and I talk with Yvonne Inghels and her daughter Monique in 1984, reminiscing about Raymond, who died years earlier. Courtesy of Marc de Waele.

Above, with Julia and Albert (Jan) Eetvelder—the "man in the turtleneck sweater." He was threatened by a policeman who suspected him of helping me. Below, Susanne Famaey. In 1943 she told her brother, the policeman, "Let him run. If you turn him in, you will not be able to live with your own family."

Despite her fear, Hedwige Proost took me into her home, shown here. Dr. Jean Proost rode his bicycle in a freezing downpour to look for an "underground connection."

Henri Malfait, my underground connection, was arrested by the Gestapo two months after I left Brussels. He is shown here as no. 48596, still in his Buchenwald prison garb but somewhat fattened three weeks after liberation.

Above, in summer 1945, Henri rejoined his parents, Thérèse and Octave Malfait, who had sheltered me. Below, in 1985 Henri and I stand in front of the very house, still occupied by the Malfaits.

Raoul Thibaut was a member of the Comet Line and of Service Zero, an intelligence arm of the Belgian resistance. His wife, Marie, who perished in a concentration camp, was posthumously awarded the Medal of Freedom by the U.S. War Department.

This identity photo, taken in Paris by a member of the Comet Line and shown actual size, got me past Gestapo control.

Above, Margie sits with Pierre and Micheline Lily Ugeux, the legendary "Michou," who personally helped rescue 150 airmen. She was awarded the U.S. Medal of Freedom with Gold Palm, the highest award presented to civilians in World War II. Pierre, working with British Intelligence, had parachuted into Nazi-occupied Europe. Below, when we visited a school in Sint-Anna, Hamme, in 1984, this ten-year-old sang "Doodle-ee-doo" in English and rolled her eyes like a Roaring Twenties flapper as classmates looked on.

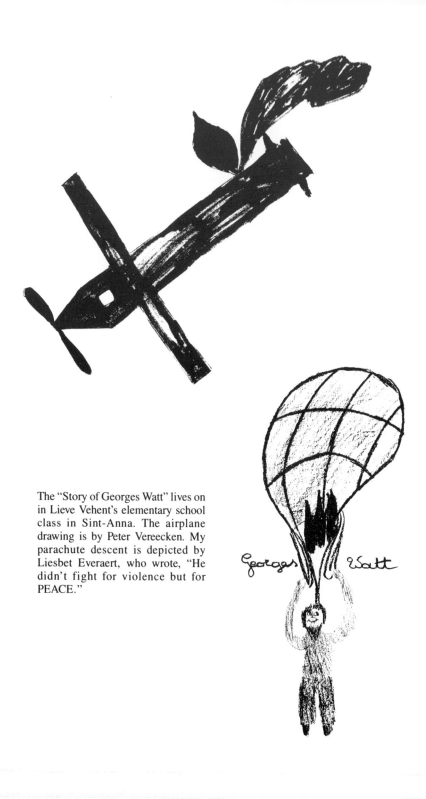

The "Story of Georges Watt" lives on in Lieve Vehent's elementary school class in Sint-Anna. The airplane drawing is by Peter Vereecken. My parachute descent is depicted by Liesbet Everaert, who wrote, "He didn't fight for violence but for PEACE."

In this drawing by Ilse Rooms of Sint-Anna, German soldiers and their dog search for me while Eduard Lauwaert and I hide in a berry bush.

While I was off at the war, Margie divided her time between riveting tail sections at an aircraft plant on Long Island and raising Danny.

Back in the States in 1944, I served as a B-17 flight engineer instructor at MacDill Field, Tampa, till the end of the war.

Above, New York, 1955. Margie and I are proud parents of Dan (holding Lefty) and Steven. Dan was 3½ when I was shot down; Steven was an early baby boomer, born November 1944. Below, Northport, Long Island, 1989. Margie and I now enjoy retirement and grand- and great-grandparenting. Photo by Breena Kaplan.

Lexington, Kentucky, 1988. Survivors of the crash reunite to enjoy a delayed "debriefing." Left to right: Current, Watt, Maiorca, Smith, Meader, and Bramwell.

The other survivors: Virginia Bramwell, Sarah Smith, Eileen Meader, Margie Watt, and Marilyn Current.

5

The Ditch and the Outhouse

I lay down gasping for breath in a dry irrigation ditch surrounded by thick shrub. Thoroughly exhausted, I settled down to sweat things out till nightfall. And sweat I did, literally. It was only midafternoon, and it felt like an unusually warm day for early November. I took off my heated suit, leaving only my summer coveralls over my long johns.

The man with the cap, who had disappeared soon after showing me where to hide, returned. When he saw the electric suit lying beside me, he insisted on taking it off my hands and hiding it. He took the suit and disappeared again.

Now I was alone—at least I thought so. But when I stuck my head up over the edge of the ditch, I saw a beautiful and most comforting sight. On the field immediately beside me a farmer was plowing with his horse. On the neighboring plot another farmer was working the field by hand. And through an opening in the trees on the other side of the dirt road, I saw a man and woman taking up their labors again.

They all went about their tasks, pretending I wasn't there. They were my new escort, protecting me as those Thunderbolts had protected our plane only an hour ago. (Only an hour ago? It seemed a lifetime!)

Now I had time to think about the next step. I knew I had to get as far away as possible from this area. Our intelligence officers had told us in briefings that during the first forty-eight hours the Germans conduct a very intensive and methodical search in the immediate area. And then, just as methodically, after forty-eight hours they discontinue the search. I was sure they were already combing the fields for me and the rest of the crew. It was dangerous to move about. With luck I could hide out in that spot till nightfall.

The next problem was how to connect with the underground. Everyone knew there was a well-organized underground. But how did you reach it? Its members operated with the utmost care and secrecy. I couldn't go around asking, "Where's the underground?" Perhaps they would come to me?

My general plan was to head for France, which, we were informed by our intelligence, was the main escape route. The German coastal buildup against the expected allied invasion across the English Channel made escape from Europe by fishing boat virtually impossible.

My spirits were up. I was trying to take in everything that had happened to me that day. It was only two-thirty in the afternoon, but the events in the morning seemed to have taken place many, many years before in some other world. Which one was the real world, I wondered.

At that moment I was actually thrilled at the idea of being here among these people. I did not know what lay ahead, but I welcomed the experience. It wasn't the danger that appealed to me but the idea of sharing the experience of people fighting Hitler's Germany. I thought of the French Maquis in the forests of southern France, of the anti-Franco guerrillas still fighting against Franco in Asturias, and of the partisans in Yugoslavia. In those few minutes I fantasized that I would somehow find my way to one of these groups.

I knew that many of the leaders of these partisan movements in the occupied countries were Spanish Republican exiles and former volunteers in the International Brigades. The experience we had gained in the Spanish war was now being put to use in the world war against Hitler. This war was only the continuation of that one. A passionate hatred of Fascism characterized those men and women who came from so many nations to fight against Hitler and Mussolini in Spain. They would never give up, no matter how hard the fight.

I hoped I would run into some of them. But I knew that my immediate duty was not to stay and fight but to make good my escape and get back to England as soon as possible. I would do my damnedest to get away. I knew that if I were captured and the Germans learned that I was a former Lincoln Brigader and a Jew, I would not fare well at their hands.

This was not the first time I had been behind enemy lines, however. In March 1938 in Spain our battalion was completely surrounded. The Fascists had already taken the main towns and were patrolling the roads. Peasants gave us food and showed us the best routes back to our own lines. It was in that experience that I learned to respect the resourcefulness of the peasant. No wonder I felt such love and respect for these villagers around me.

As I lay in that ditch thinking about the next steps, I began to realize that what had seemed like a mild November day was in fact a cold November day. The chill was beginning to move into my bones, and I was sorry that I had gotten rid of my leather flight jacket and my electric suit. I was becoming aware of a pain in my back. I tried lying on my back in the bottom of the ditch, but the dampness only made it worse. I realized also I had not eaten since six-thirty that morning.

And so, as I began to feel the physical effects of the day—fatigue, hunger, backache, and cold—my euphoria gave way to a more realistic fear. I kept wishing that someone would come along to take my mind off the pain and cold.

Someone did come along—the man who had originally shown me to my hiding place and who had taken my electric suit, the man with the cap. I watched him as he approached me stealthily, taking advantage of every bit of natural cover the earth offered. It had taken months of infantry training for me to learn how to infiltrate hostile terrain. The farmer comes by the skill naturally. He has a native shrewdness about the land. He knows every nook and cranny, every blade of grass. No wonder he makes such a good soldier and scout in the army.

"Bonjour," he said as he slipped into the trench beside me. "I hid your suit. No one will find it. When you come back here to this town, I will give it to you again."

"Oh, that isn't necessary," I said. "Make something out of it. Keep it for yourself. I'll get another."

He was insistent and said he would give it to no one else but me. Not to the general of the Allied armies and not even to the supply sergeant. Thinking how powerful supply sergeants are, I laughed and thanked him, promising to return someday to get it. My companion was a man of few words and did not tarry long after this brief exchange.

Soon after he left, I spotted two men approaching my hiding place. One was dressed in a suit with a white shirt and tie and hat. The other was wearing a turtleneck sweater. As I welcomed them into my "home," I recognized the suited fellow as one of the people who had been talking to the *gendarme*. I had imagined, though I wasn't quite sure, that he was telling the policeman to turn me over to the Germans. So I was wary of him. Yet if he were out to betray me, why had he come here? He could easily have told the Germans where I was hiding, since he obviously knew where I was. But I kept my guard up just the same and let him do the talking at first.

Speaking in passable English, he told me that I had escaped not a minute too soon. Immediately after I had left the spot, the "Black Brigades" (Belgian pro-Nazis) had arrived and asked everyone where I had gone. No one knew. Someone volunteered that I had run off in the direction opposite the one in which I had fled.

My informant was a seaman named Raymond Inghels. His friend in the turtleneck was Jan Van Eetvelder. "New York is my second home," Raymond said. "I sailed to New York forty times.

I was chef on a ship. But now I must work as a cook for the Germans in Antwerp."

Raymond had been home on shore leave when the Nazis invaded Belgium, he told me. He set out to return to his ship, which was anchored in Rouen, but when he arrived in France, the authorities—angered by Belgium's capitulation to the Germans and mistaking him for a naval officer in his blue merchant marine uniform—arrested him. Raymond managed to escape.

He was soon captured again, this time by the Germans. After a few days in captivity he succeeded in persuading the Germans to let him go. He even wangled a bicycle out of them and headed back toward Belgium. But he was captured a second time. Then one day, as the Germans were escorting a group of prisoners to another site, Raymond and a few others made a break for it. The Germans opened fire as the prisoners scrambled across the field into a wooded area. Raymond's suitcase was shredded, and his shoes were torn by the bullets, but he got away. He ditched his uniform, picked up some old clothes and a pair of torn house slippers from a farmer, and made it all the way back to Brussels on foot.

Raymond knew how to spin a yarn. He told the story with zest and humor, and it endeared him to me. But I was already disposed to like him because he was a seaman. Ever since I fought alongside them in the Spanish Civil War, I've had a soft spot for seamen. As a group they were among the most courageous. I enjoyed their humor and romantic sentimentality; I admired—even envied—their irreverence toward authority.

Raymond and I talked about a lot of things—about how the war was going, about our mutual hatred of the Germans, about conditions in Germany and in Belgium, about the Moscow Conference, about New York and Long Island, about the Flying Fortress and the Luftwaffe.

Our conversation was interrupted several times by the droning of a low-flying plane that passed repeatedly overhead. I assumed the pilot was looking for me and the other crew members. We ducked our heads and made sure that our faces and hands were not visible to the pilot—a practice I had learned as an infantryman in Spain.

The three of us were still sitting around talking when I spotted a farmer approaching us. I had wanted company before, but four of us in that narrow ditch? That was a little too much of a crowd, and dangerous, I thought. He made himself immediately welcome, however, when he pulled a sandwich out of a bag and handed it to me. Food at last! It was an egg sandwich with real honest-to-goodness eggs, not the powdered "wooden eggs" the air force cooks dished up—except when we were preparing to fly a mission. ("The condemned men ate a hearty breakfast," we used to say.)

The man just sat there and smiled at me as I devoured the food. He spoke a few words in Flemish to Raymond, who turned to me and asked, "Do you know this man?"

"He looks familiar," I said.

"He is the man on whose field you fell."

I took another look. Of course. He was the "stump." I shook his hand and smiled and thanked him. The farmer spoke to my friend again.

Raymond asked me, "Do you know what he is saying? He is saying that all the villagers are calling you *l'Ange blanc*, the White Angel. You descended from the sky. You have brought us good tidings. You are an omen of the coming liberation of our people." Raymond added that the farmer was the envy of all the other farmers in the area because it was on his land that the *aviateur* had fallen, and that made him something special.

I thanked him again for the sandwich. He went away very pleased.

My new friend asked me if I had any plans for escape. By now I felt I could trust him, but I really had no plans. All I knew was that I had to get as far away as possible from that area and head for France. He asked me if I had any means of contacting anyone who could help me. I told him no, that so far I was going it alone.

"I will help you," he said. "Tonight, after dark, I will bring you some clothes, and I will buy a railroad ticket for you. You can't speak Flemish, and they would catch you at the station." Apparently he was not connected with the organized underground and was doing this on his own. I had hoped for an agent of the resistance, but it was the best offer I'd had all day.

"Okay," I said.

We were interrupted by a soft whistle blowing across the field. Then another. It was a danger signal. Raymond quickly repeated his promise to return that night, and the two men scurried down the ditch and disappeared from sight.

I moved to a more protected spot a few yards away and waited for the search parties to pass by. I could hear voices, shouts, dogs barking, which told me the Germans were quite close. Then I saw three German soldiers cycling down the road along which that "country squire" had told me to hide. I most certainly would have had it if I had followed his advice!

I now settled down again to wait for dark. It was taking so long. Why didn't that sun go down? Long ago in combat I had learned that darkness can be your best friend. How I longed for it now. Time dragged on, and with the company gone the cold started to bother me once again. I tried to sleep. But the cold and the pain in my back, and fear, kept me awake. Why didn't the night come?

Slowly, very slowly, the sun moved toward the horizon. A man and a woman came walking down the road. He was several paces in front of her and kept whistling a tune. They walked past my hiding place, talked to one of the farmers on the other side of the field, then quickly ducked down and made their way toward me.

It was several hours since I had come down, and I thought perhaps by now some agent of the underground had gotten wind of my whereabouts. I scrutinized these two very carefully. They were fairly young. The man looked more like a worker than a peasant. The woman wore glasses and seemed alert and intelligent. They fit my mental image of underground agents.

We exchanged greetings in French. Then the man, speaking English, asked, "Will you come to our house to eat with us?" The unusual fact that he spoke English and invited me to their home reinforced the idea that they might be the people I was looking for. Still, I hesitated. I had to think this through. I felt I could trust them, but I wasn't sure they were connected with the organized resistance, and I already had one definite arrangement in hand. I had made a commitment to meet Raymond after dark. He would help me; I was sure of that. He was probably already preparing the clothes and working out the plans for my escape. No use swapping horses in midstream.

I made up my mind to stick with Raymond. So I politely declined their invitation. They didn't quite understand why and persisted in asking me. When I told them I was already taken care of, they seemed to understand and quickly took their leave of me. Again, the man walked ahead whistling while the woman followed several paces behind.

The way they departed convinced me all the more that they were probably the ones I should have gone with. If I had yielded to my better judgment I would have accepted their offer. But I thought of that seaman and the risks he would take to get to me. So sentiment and not intuition prevailed.

I lay down to shiver again. It was dusk now. The faithful farmer and his horse came around to me again. We shook hands and said goodbye. The farmer on the other side left soon after. They could not stay past their usual work time without arousing suspicion. Again there was that sense of aloneness that I had felt when the P-47s left us earlier that day.

It was not quite dark when another man came walking quickly to my hiding place. I recognized him as one of the long procession that had visited the field earlier. He was excited and spoke so rapidly in Flemish that I had to slow him down. When I made him repeat what he had said, I was able to grasp that more soldiers had arrived and were now heading toward me. I must get away at once.

I tried to tell him in French, in German, and with body motions that I didn't want to leave that spot, that it was as good as any in the dark, and that I had an arrangement to meet someone. He became more agitated and insisted upon my leaving at once. Another villager soon joined us and made the same pitch.

I was beginning to be persuaded when the man with the cap came up. He was wearing a corduroy jacket. He saw me shivering from the cold, removed his coat, and handed it me. It felt really good. After a hurried exchange with the others, the man with the cap said, "You must go with them at once." That clinched the matter.

One of the men remained behind while I walked swiftly away with the other two. We were halfway across the field when the man behind us whistled to the others, and they broke into a run, with me limping right behind them, for a considerable distance. There was still some faint light, and silhouettes were still visible from afar.

We stopped behind a clump of bushes. When the third man caught up with us, they held a muffled conversation that I couldn't understand. Then one turned and handed me a paper bag with meat and a bottle of beer, which I stuffed into the pockets of the corduroy jacket. "This is for the trip," the man with the cap said. I said goodbye to the two farmers and went off with the man with the cap.

We covered about two kilometers, cutting across fields and ditches and country roads. Whenever we came to a road, my guide would stop, crouch close to the ground, and look up and down in both directions before he let me cross. Once again I marveled at the caution and skill of the farmer in using the terrain.

It was fully dark as we came into a village. We passed through a farmyard and backyards of houses and along a high wall that separated us from the road. I could see no one, but occasionally I heard a motorcycle or car racing along on the opposite side of the wall.

We finally came through a little gate into a cobblestone yard. My guide took off his wooden shoes and held his finger to his lips to warn me to go silently. Then he ushered me through a door into complete darkness, telling me to wait until he came back for me.

It certainly was dark there, but no darkness could hide the odor of that room. It didn't take any brilliant deduction to tell me I was in an outhouse. In all the escape stories I had read or seen in the movies there were haystacks and closets, attics and barns, even pickle barrels—but I couldn't remember an outhouse.

I waited a long time, it seemed. Then I heard footsteps across the yard. Out of caution I went deeper into the shadow against the stone wall. A young man and woman opened the door. At first they didn't see me. When I stepped out of the shadow, their bewildered looks turned into bright smiles. They explained that I had to wait a little longer until they put *der kleine*, the little one, to bed. Then I could come into their house.

So again I waited for what seemed an even longer and colder time. Finally the woman came back, this time alone, and led me into her house.

6

Birthday Party in Hamme

As the door closed behind me, I felt at long last the relief of being inside a warm house. It seemed years since I had been indoors, and still longer since I had been in a home. Those four walls of that large Belgian kitchen were like the walls of a fortress, protecting me from the cold and the danger lurking outside.

The young woman sat me down beside the huge Belgian stove that jutted out into the room. While I was thawing out, she was already dishing up potatoes and getting out beer for me. I could see now that as long as I was cared for by these kind Flemish farmers, I would not want for food. I was told that soon a man who could speak German would come by, and our conversation would be easier. The man with the cap left the room—on some errand, I assumed.

A little man with a big handlebar mustache and a mischievous grin soon breezed in. It was impossible to tell his age; he could have been forty-five or he could have been sixty. His energy was boundless. He jumped about that room like a little elf. He talked and joked, and cursed the *boche* with great relish. He welcomed me as if I were a long-lost son.

He spoke German well enough, and after we got through the preliminaries of how soon the Allied forces would arrive in Belgium, he said, "Don't worry. You are safe now. We will save you. The *patrioten* will help you escape."

I told him I was confident in them and had no fears.

"But you must be careful," the old man said. "You know what would happen to you if you got caught? They would just throw

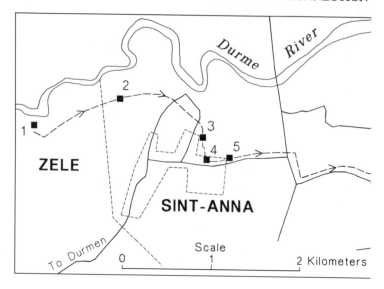

you in prison camp. Do you know what would happen to us? It would be *kaput*." He drew his hand across his neck in emphasis. But then he danced over to the stove, picked up a knife, and said with a gleam in his eye, "If the *boche* comes in here, I'll take this knife and cut his throat, like this."

I laughed and nodded agreement. This only encouraged the old man. He was getting more and more worked up and kept repeating. "I'll cut his throat out," laughing and winking with each sweep of the knife.

A middle-aged couple came in. At first I thought they were neighbors, but I soon learned that they were the parents of Eduard Lauwaert, the man with the cap. The senior Lauwaert, like the little old guy, Leon Ducolumbeir, was a veteran of World War I. We sat around the stove and talked about the last war and how the present war was going, about the Moscow Conference, about the exciting advances of the Russians. The conversation was part French, part German, with Ducolumbeir acting as interpreter when needed.

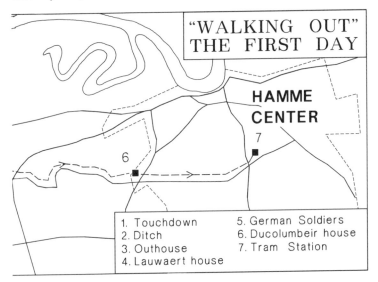

"WALKING OUT" THE FIRST DAY

HAMME CENTER

1. Touchdown
2. Ditch
3. Outhouse
4. Lauwaert house
5. German Soldiers
6. Ducolumbeir house
7. Tram Station

As I fed them news of the goings-on in the world, I realized that they were remarkably well informed. I asked them how they came to know all these things. They smiled, very pleased with themselves, and said, "We listen to the radio broadcasts from London every night."

"But isn't it illegal to own a radio?"

"It's not illegal to own a radio. It's just illegal to tune in on the British *poste*," they answered. "If we get caught, we are taken away by the Gestapo. In the beginning, many people were caught. The Germans would shut off the power and rush into homes while the lights were out. It they found the radio dials set at the BBC, they would arrest every member of the family. But we have learned how to deal with this. As soon as the power is cut off, we're prepared to turn the dial back to another station. Now they do not catch us anymore."

A loud knock on the front door scared the daylights out of me. The old man pointed to the back door, and I was out of there in no seconds flat, hiding in the shadows in the yard. I wasn't there long before Eduard's wife, Mathilde, came out and led me back into the house. She explained that she ran a small grocery store in the front room of the house, and a man had come to buy something, but she had sent him away, telling him the store was closed.

After we settled down again, they talked about the difficulties of life under the occupation. Lauwaert had a small ropemaking business, but because his son Eduard refused to "volunteer" to work for the Germans, they did not allow the Lauwaerts to run the family business. Eduard was also prevented from working at his trade as a flaxer.

One day Eduard came to his father saying he had been asked to join the Vlaams Nationaal Verbond, a Flemish nationalist organization that supported the German occupation. If he signed up, he would be able to work.

"I told him, 'No, don't join,'" Lauwaert said. "My son said, 'Now listen, Dad. You don't have to sign. I will sign up and still stay with the resistance. In the meantime we could work.' I said to him, 'Now you listen. I have only one son, and that is you. If you sign with the VNV, you are no longer my son. I know you don't have any work, but if you don't have enough food for your wife and child, we will find food for you.' My son didn't sign, and I am proud of him."

Life was made very difficult for the Lauwaerts. They had to scrape by on family savings, vegetables raised in their small backyard, Eduard's odd jobs, and Mathilde's part-time work for a wheat farmer, plus the small grocery store in their house.

Eduard was a member of the Belgian Volunteer League, the resistance organization in Zele, Hamme, and Dendermonde. Once, while he was carrying out an intelligence assignment at the military airport in Waasmunster, a German soldier with two dogs came toward him. He kept under cover, but the dogs picked up his scent, and the German soldier headed in his direction. Eduard fired at the German and barely got away.

Mathilde worked alongside Eduard in the resistance. They distributed an illegal newspaper. One day the Germans came to search their house. Mathilde had the newspapers hidden inside a pile of underwear.

"The Germans pulled out the drawer that held the underwear," Mathilde related. "They were standing there with the newspapers actually in their hands. We were frightened, sure they would discover the papers. But they put the drawer back, closed the curtain, and left."

The Lauwaerts and Ducolumbeir asked me questions about the bombing raids, the fate of the crew, and what it was like up there above 30,000 feet. I went over the day's events. They kept laughing at the coup they had pulled off, snatching an American airman from under the noses of the "supermen."

In the course of the conversation I let slip that it was my thirtieth birthday. Their eyes opened wide; they laughed and said I was really lucky. "You have received the best birthday present," Lauwaert said. "You are alive, and you are safe with us." My hostess scurried excitedly about the kitchen, and suddenly bread, sausage, and beer appeared from secret hiding places. Then the festivities really commenced.

They kept repeating over and over how lucky I was, what a wonderful omen it was for them and for me, how everything was going to be all right. The old man was flying higher than ever. He kept us in stitches with his pantomimes of what he would do to the Germans if they came into his house. I could still hear the German cars, motorcycles, and trucks racing down the street just outside the door—a sound that didn't dampen the mood of the birthday party but had a sobering effect on me.

In the midst of the partying Eduard reappeared, carrying some civilian clothes—a dark shiny pinstriped suit, a vest, a scarf, and a pair of worn-out black shoes. There was no shirt and no hat.

"Put these on," he said. "You must get ready to leave at once."

I took off my coveralls and the electrically heated boots I was still wearing and dressed hurriedly in the alcove next to the room. I looked at myself in the small mirror on the wall. Could I pass as a Belgian, I wondered? My new friends seemed pleased at the transformation.

Eduard asked me if I had any money. I showed him my escape kit, which held chocolate bars, malt tablets, two silk handkerchief maps of western Europe, an "anal" compass (named for its hiding place), and two hundred francs.

He took one look at the francs and to my surprise uttered an expletive in Flemish. Then, with exasperation, he said in French, "These francs are no good! They're of no use in Belgium. You need Belgian francs. Why didn't they give you Belgian francs?"

He seemed very upset as he tore out of the room. He came back shortly and handed me four hundred Belgian francs.

"You will leave at once with the old man." He said. "He will take you to his house."

Ducolumbeir looked at me gleefully and winked, as if to say, "You are in good hands."

I hated to go. Getting out of there was like leaving the loving protection of the foxhole to run through machine-gun fire and an artillery barrage. No matter how many times I had gone over the top in combat, I had always felt that sinking feeling in the pit of my stomach just before every action. I was to face that same feeling again whenever the time came for me to leave one haven for another.

Mathilde went out first to see if the coast was clear. The old man and I then stepped into the cool crisp air, and the door closed quickly behind us. It was still early evening, but the streets were empty. The moon was already up and bright. The stone houses on both sides of the road stood in ghostly silence in the blackout. Only the old man's wooden shoes, clattering on the cobblestones, echoed eerily through the silent air. I was shivering, partly from cold—the threadbare suit jacket without a shirt was not warm enough—and partly from fear, I'm sure. I imagined that anyone could see I didn't belong.

But my spine tingled with excitement. Adventure was there, and there is no adventure without some fear. I tried to absorb my surroundings, to fix that scene forever in my memory.

The old man beside me seemed not to worry. As we walked down the street he kept talking (too loudly I thought). He pointed to each house we passed, commenting, *"Dort wohnen patrioten. Dort wohnen die Schwarte.* There live the patriots; there live the Black Brigades. We know every one of them. We will take care of these traitors after the liberation."

Off in the distance ahead of us I thought I heard the persistent sound of water passing over a millwheel. The sound grew louder as we continued walking.

Suddenly, it wasn't water over a mill. It was the clatter of horses' hoofs on the cobblestone pavement. They were coming toward us! "It's a cavalry patrol coming back from the search," I thought. Closer and closer they came. I glanced anxiously at the old man and pointed urgently to a dark alley we were just passing: "Let's hide here."

The old man was disturbingly undisturbed.

"No," he said. "Just remember. *Nicht sprechen.* Let me do all the talking."

I thought he was crazy. Why take a chance? But I could not show him I was afraid. Besides, he was leading me, and I knew I would follow him. So I gulped down my fear and accepted his decision. But I couldn't keep my heart from pounding.

Suddenly the object of my fears loomed before us. Two truck horses were pulling an old World War I army wagon. It had an arch over the top, and in the driver's seat were three German soldiers. Impulsively, I swung around to the left of the old man, to be on the outside of the road. There was no ducking out now. No hiding in alleys and no running away. Slowly and irresistibly the wagon came toward us, making a godawful racket on the pavement.

The old man broke into spirited conversation with me, speaking in Flemish, of course. He could have been talking of this year's crop or of the weather, for all I knew or cared. Not only couldn't I understand the language, but I was not listening to him. I was concentrating on my feet. "Keep walking," I said to myself. "Keep putting one foot in front of the other. Don't run. Don't turn away. Don't panic now. You'll ruin everything. Look them straight in the eye."

I could almost see their eyes now. Goddam that moon! It's always there when you don't want it. Why is that end man over there looking at me like that? Could he be . . . ? Cut it out, you're getting panicky. He can't tell you're no Belgian. Boy, am I glad I didn't get that haircut! I look less GI this way.

"Guten Abend," the old man said to them.

I nodded my head in greeting.

"Guten Abend," the "superman" said.

Guten Abend. You dirty bastards, you poor dumb bastards! You've searched the fields all afternoon. You're looking for me everywhere. Here I am. Right in your hands. You dumb bastards, letting me slip right through your fingers!

Now they passed us. I wanted to look around. I wanted to run. I found myself instinctively quickening my pace. With a supreme effort of will I slowed down. I felt the eyes of that end guy staring at my back. My ears were tuned to the receding clatter of the horses. They didn't stop. They didn't turn back.

I looked at the old man. He winked at me with his whole face. I smiled back at him with my face, but my heart was laughing.

Suddenly he nudged me into an alley.

"What are we going to do now?" I asked.

"Pissen," he said with a pixyish wink.

I was never so glad to *pissen* in all my life!

7

The Policeman
and the Parachute

We still had some three or four kilometers to go before arriving at Ducolumbeir's house, but it didn't matter. I was no longer cold. I was no longer afraid. Even my ankle didn't bother me. We had left the cluster of houses in Sint-Anna, a hamlet in Hamme, where we had met the Germans. Now the road led across a long stretch of open fields. In the bright moonglow the countryside looked like a Renaissance landscape. It was beautiful. I was feeling great.

In Hamme proper, tightly packed rows of attached houses lined both sides of the street. Again, the noise of the old man's wooden shoes echoed off the walls and made me a bit nervous.

At last we arrived at his house. We entered through a narrow hallway into a large kitchen, again with an enormous Belgian stove jutting into the middle of the room.

A tall, stocky, attractive woman, looking considerably younger than her husband, greeted us as if we were expected. How did she know we were coming? Why did she not show surprise or fear at seeing me? I marveled again at the courage of these villagers and at the efficiency of their grapevine.

The table was set with bread and black sausage. Food was the last thing I wanted. I had eaten in the field and again when I first came in from the outhouse and then again at the birthday party. But I could not insult my hosts. I ate.

We went over the day's events. The old man left the room and returned with a small mimeographed newspaper called the *Patriot,* printed in Flemish and French. He told me with pride that it was issued by the local resistance.

Now fatigue was setting in, and I struggled to stay awake. My hosts saw me fighting to keep my eyes open and mercifully showed me to a room on a higher level, with an inside window that looked down on the kitchen. On the bed was an old-fashioned down cover and a mattress that you could sink into forever. As the soft down enveloped me, I felt heavenly comfort such as I had not known since my early childhood.

I was thoroughly exhausted and thought I would fall asleep immediately. But the softness and warmth of the bed only sharpened the pain in my back and ankle. All my muscles felt sore. Then the events of that unbelievable day began to race through my mind—the fire in Number One engine, the German fighter with his shell bursts and tracers racing toward me, the plane going down out of control. I imagined myself alternately blowing up with the plane or jumping without my chute, hurtling nightmarishly toward the ground.

I wondered what had happened to the rest of the crew. I had seen only seven chutes open. I kept trying to remember whether I had counted my own in the seven. Two or three men must have gone down with the ship—it was painful to speculate which ones.

I thought of Raymond Inghels and wondered whether he would know what had happened to me, and whether I would ever see him again. I felt as if I had stood him up and mentally apologized to him. I thought about that couple whose invitation I had turned down and wondered whether I had made the right decision. All of this was keeping me awake.

Finally, I fell into a deep sleep. It seemed only a moment later that I was being vigorously shaken. As I reluctantly reached consciousness, I became aware of someone speaking English.

"Wake up, Georges!" Raymond stood over me, happy and triumphant.

Raymond! I was overjoyed. How did he find me? How comforting to see him. Eduard Lauwaert was there with him. What was their connection?

As I rose to shake Raymond's hand, a sharp pain shot through my back. Raymond noticed my grimace. I told him I had hurt my back when the chute opened. He said he would massage my back and, despite my protests, proceeded to do so.

While he worked, he talked rapidly and excitedly about the events of the day before. He said he had come back with some clothes after dark to the spot where he had left me.

"I was calling, 'Georges. Georges.' You did not answer. I looked every place and kept calling you. I could not find you. I was very upset. I did not know what to do."

He had returned to the village and searched everywhere. His persistence led him finally to Eduard Lauwaert.

"I had to convince him to let me come along to help you," Raymond said.

As I began to dress, I looked for my dogtags, then remembered putting them into a pocket of my fatigues, which I had given to Lauwaert when I changed clothes. I told Eduard that it would be extremely dangerous for me to be caught without any identification. I could be shot as a spy. Without a moment's hesitation, he said he would get them for me. He borrowed a bike from the old man and rode the four kilometers back to his home in Sint-Anna.

While we were waiting, Raymond continued to relate the events of the day before. After he and his friend Jan left me, he had gone home to find his wife in tears. Their house was in a shambles. The Germans had been there and had torn everything out of closets, ripped beds, and destroyed furniture. They had searched for me in houses throughout the village, leaving utter devastastion in their wake.

After dark, when he was getting ready to leave his house, he told me his wife burst into tears again and said she knew where he was going. It was too dangerous. He should think of his wife and children.

"You know what I told her, Georges? I said, 'I must go. I gave my word. I cannot live with myself if I don't help him.' From the very beginning I knew I was going to help you. Do you know what I said to the policeman, Georges? I told him you were an American *aviateur,* and he should turn you over to the Germans. Do you know why I said that, Georges?"

I said nothing.

"So the traitors in the crowd would not suspect that I was going to help you. But from the very first moment I saw you, I knew I would help save you. And you see, now I am here."

He also reported the rumor that five members of my crew, landing on the other side of the river, had been immediately captured by the Germans. One of the men was believed to be wounded. Raymond had no knowledge of the others.

He then told me what happened between the Belgian *gendarme* and his Nazi boss when the policeman brought in my parachute. Raymond acted out the scene between them with dramatic gusto, taking the role of each in turn.

"What have you got there?" demanded the German commander.

"A parachute, sir."

"Yes, yes, I can see that. I'm not blind. Where did you get it?"

"In the field near the river."

"Why did you bring the parachute? I'm not interested in the parachute. Where is the parachutist?"

"I don't know, sir."

"What do you mean, you don't know? You let him get away!"

"I didn't see him," the policeman protested.

"Who helped him?" The irate Nazi was fuming now.

"I don't know."

"What do you mean you don't know? Weren't there people at the spot where he fell? You must have recognized someone."

"Yes, but I don't know who helped him."

"You've lived in this village all your life and you don't know who they were?"

"There were so many of them. The whole village was there," lamented the cop.

The German officer was getting angrier and angrier, turning red and purple with rage.

"We will have that parachutist!" he shouted at the Belgian. "If he is not found in one hour's time, I will take every man, woman, and child in this village and have them shot!"

Raymond was a born actor. He ended the story with a flourish and a loud guffaw, his cheeks actually becoming the colors he attributed to the Nazi.

Raymond then turned his attention to me and said, "The Germans are everywhere in the villages around here. They are watching the railroad station. It is too dangerous to go by train. They will also be guarding the tram station, but that is less dangerous than the train. I will take you to the tram before daylight and buy the ticket for you. Then you will ride to Antwerp. What are your plans after that?"

I repeated what I had told him the day before. My plans were to head for Paris and try to contact the underground. I had no clear idea beyond that.

Raymond thought for a moment. Then he said he had a brother-in-law and sister-in-law in Brussels. The man was a doctor who perhaps could help me. He would give me the address.

I was grateful for the offer and thanked Raymond. But now, for the first time, I was confronted with the practical reality of my situation, and I began to realize how extremely dangerous it was.

First, I'd have to memorize the names and the address and all the minute details of directions, what trains, what trams to take, where and how to change trams or trains, how to purchase tickets, how to get to a toilet, how to get food once I ran out of the malt tablets in my escape kit.

And what about a total stranger, speaking very poor French, knocking on the door of a couple in Brussels and saying, "Raymond sent me?" Why would they trust me? With a justifiable instinct for self-preservation they could figure I was a German spy trying to entrap them. Or they could simply be afraid to get involved. The consequence of being caught helping an American flyer was death.

Raymond must have been reading my mind, for no sooner had we settled on this plan then he said, "Georges, it's too dangerous for you. How will you find the address in a strange place where you don't even know the language? How do I know that my brother-in-law will take you in? No, I cannot let you do this by yourself. I will go with you to my relatives."

"It's too dangerous for you, Raymond," I protested. "You have done enough. I have to chance this alone."

"I cannot let you do this alone," Raymond insisted. "How can I even have such an idea? I cannot live with myself if I let you go alone. There. It's settled. I am going with you, Georges."

I protested again, but this time with a little less conviction, and finally accepted his offer. I was considerably relieved.

Eduard returned with my dogtags. I thanked him and said I needed only one, which I hid in my shoe. "When you get to London," he said, "tell them my name. Don't forget. Eduard Lauwaert, from the village of Hamme. I am a member of the Belgian Volunteer League."

"I won't forget what you did for me, and I won't forget to tell them about you," I said as I vigorously shook his hand. "Goodbye, Eduard."

There was no time left now, for we had to get to the tram before daylight. I said a grateful goodbye to the old man and his wife and once again stepped out of a warm comfortable haven into the fearful unknown.

Eduard left the house first. Raymond and I followed about thirty paces behind. It was still dark, but unlike the night before, the street was alive with people on bicycles and on foot, hurrying to work. This time I felt comfortable in the crowd.

On the way we encountered a company of German soldiers marching in formation toward us. In the narrow street I had to hug the walls to keep from brushing up against them. Yet I wasn't frightened. Was I getting used to them?

We arrived at a busy intersection. Raymond signaled for me to wait in the shadow of a small chapel while he went to buy the tickets. Eduard, who had been keeping a discreet distance, now came over to me, shook my hand warmly, and departed quickly before Raymond came back with the tickets.

Raymond and I walked separately toward the tram.

8

On the Tram

I felt very strange in that early morning tram. Belgian trams were nothing like American streetcars. The seats were arranged in compartments, so you sat facing other passengers all the time. That's what made me so uncomfortable. These were workingmen on their way to work. They carried their lunches in bags and boxes. In that dim pre-dawn light I imagined that some of them were staring at me with too much curiosity. What would it be like when the sun came up?

Raymond was sitting in a compartment on the other side facing me. I could see the barely perceptible lines of excitement on his face. The tram gradually began to come to life, and passengers were talking across the rows and aisles. I pretended sleep, but curiosity forced my eyes open from time to time.

The dawn came slowly. Gray frost lay heavy on the fields between the towns, and the cold dampness penetrated the car. The crowd began to thin out as passengers got off at successive stops. Raymond, who was getting bolder and bolder by the minute, began winking and smiling at me. When the window seat opposite me became vacant, he moved into it.

Several times Germans in uniform boarded the car, rode for a while, and got off. Some stood on the outer platform, which was separated from the inside of the car by a glass partition. Even I was getting bolder and more assured. When I found myself looking directly through the window at a German soldier who was standing on the street looking at me, I did not turn my glance away from him. It was as if the glass of the window were enough to protect me from my enemy.

The tram came to a stop opposite a huge soccer field where several platoons of German soldiers were going through some sort of close-order drill. A squad stood at attention. At the command of the drillmaster they broke ranks and scattered across the field. Then, in response to a whistle, they stopped dead in their tracks, wheeled about, rushed back into formation, and snapped to attention again. They did this once, then again, and then again, repeating the same movement over and over.

It looked very comical to me. I stole a glance at Raymond and saw that he was also watching them intently with a slightly amused look on his face. He looked at me and winked. I looked around the car and saw that everyone was watching the drill and exchanging glances. I realized that the gyrations of the soldiers looked just as funny to them as they did to me.

Someone made a remark, and everyone laughed. More talk and laughter ensued. It didn't take long for Raymond to find his cue. I knew what was coming but was powerless to stop him. Raymond began to talk.

Well, he told them everything. How the day before an American plane went down near his hometown. How seven chutes opened up. How the American parachutists were all captured except one. He told of the German search parties sent out to comb the fields. He told of their ransacking homes and barns, searching everywhere, but being unable to find the missing *aviateur*.

The riders listened in rapt attention and exchanged glances with smiles of satisfaction and delight on their faces. I listened with mounting fear that someone might make the connection with me. I tried sending warning signals to Raymond but couldn't get through. He had center stage and wasn't going to relinquish it. A heavy-set man with a dark mustache started to say something, but he didn't have a chance. Raymond, who sensed the drama and the response of his audience, was not to be silenced or interrupted now.

He proceeded to tell them the story about the Belgian constable. Speaking in his own language, Raymond enacted the scene with even greater flair and drama than he had that morning when he struggled to tell it to me in English. The people were eating it up. They laughed at every gesture. By the time he got to the final apoplectic outburst of the German officer, the laughter ran loud and uncontrolled throughout the tram. I laughed along with them, but I was scared. Raymond was going too far, I thought.

The car was still stalled opposite that football field, and the Germans were still going through the same routine that had touched off this whole episode.

Raymond waited for the laughter to die down, then started talking again. I cursed him under my breath: "For Chrisakes, Raymond, why don't you shut up? Enough is enough." But I couldn't say a word to him.

"Do you know how high a *forteresse volante* flies?"

They shook their heads.

"Ten thousand meters!"

Raymond let this impressive bit of information sink in. Then he was ready with another.

"Do you know how cold it is up there?"

Pause.

"Fifty degrees below zero."

"Do you know how many bombs, they carry?"

"How many *aviateurs* in the crew?"

"How many bombers fly in one raid?"

Bit by bit he was feeding back to them everything I had told him the day before. There was no stopping him. Not until the tram finally moved away from the spot and the conversation turned to other topics was I able to breathe normally again.

Several hours later when we were in a position to talk freely, Raymond asked me:

"Do you know what I said to the people in the tram, Georges?"

"I know."

"I told them the whole story of what happened to you yesterday. There is only one thing I did not tell them."

"I know what that is."

"I did not point to you and say, 'You are the one.'"

"I know," I said, resisting the temptation to add, "It's a wonder you didn't."

But Raymond was hastening to apologize for this apparent slight to me. "You see, if I had pointed to you and said, 'Here sitting in the tram in front of me is the parachutist,' all the people in the car would look at you in wonder and admiration. And if a German or 'Black Brigader' had come into the car, they might have kept on looking at you and given you away."

"Thanks," I said. But I thought, "What wonderful faith is this in the people, that he knew not one of them would have turned me in!"

Raymond, I completely forgive you. Raymond, I love you.

The tram stopped at the entrance to a tunnel under the Schelde River that led to the Antwerp railroad station. There Raymond bought two tickets for the train to Brussels. Again we boarded separately but within view of each other. In about an hour we arrived in Brussels.

As we walked down the wide boulevard toward our destination, I asked Raymond, "Does your sister-in-law know I'm coming?"

"No," he said.

"Well, don't you think you ought to go in first and ask her if she'll receive me? After all, it's very dangerous for her to hide an American flyer."

"Oh, no. You will come with me. She will be very glad to have you. Watch her face. Will she be surprised when I tell her who you are!"

"Yeah. Will she be surprised," I repeated, with only the slightest hint of skepticism in my tone.

Raymond rang the bell of a modest but fashionable three-story dwelling. A young, attractive woman opened the door and, at the sight of Raymond, smiled broadly and kissed him on both cheeks. I closed the door behind us and stood awkwardly waiting for the introduction. "This is Hedwige Proost." As she glanced questionably at me, Raymond, speaking in Flemish, did the honors.

"Do you know who this is?" He was beaming. I felt like rushing out the door before he dropped the bombshell. "Georges is an American parachutist who dropped on our village yesterday."

Fear, amazement, uncertainty struggled for a moment in her eyes. Raymond was too happy and too pleased with himself to notice that look. His enthusiasm was infectious; she recovered quickly and ushered us into the kitchen, closing the door at once. But it is the first look in her eyes that I will always remember when I think of the heroism of a young doctor's wife who was afraid, yet risked her life to rescue a complete stranger.

Raymond narrated the story to her while she fixed us something to eat. We were cold and hungry, and that aroma of cooking in a modern kitchen, very much like home, warmed me all up inside.

We sat down to a bowl of potatoes and some slices of bacon. The bacon seemed practically raw, and try as I might, I couldn't get up much appetite for it.

"What's the matter, Georges? Aren't you hungry?" Raymond asked.

"Oh, er . . . no," I lied.

"I know what the trouble is." Turning to Hedwige he said, in

Flemish, "In America they fry the bacon." And to me, "My sister will fry the bacon for you."

"Don't bother," I said meekly and thought, Raymond, you came through again.

It didn't taste bad at all once it was fried.

The doctor was out making his rounds. We waited in the kitchen several hours for him to show up. Raymond kept rubbing his hands with glee at the surprise he had in store for his brother-in-law. We exchanged our life stories once again. I told him about Danny and Margie, about our home in Long Island—which I had never seen, because Margie had moved there after I had gone overseas. Raymond showed me pictures of himself, his wife, and his two beautiful children.

"New York is my second home," Raymond said. "Forty-five times I sailed to New York. After the war I will come to visit you on Long Island"

"Please. You must. My wife and I will be glad to have you. And so will my son."

"Give me your address. I will write you a letter as soon as we are freed from the Germans."

I hesitated, saying I thought it was very dangerous for him to have my address. If caught with it, how could he explain it? He poohpoohed the idea, telling me not to worry. So I gave him the address, but not without misgivings.

The doorbell rang. Raymond and the doctor's wife went to the door, while I stayed hidden in the kitchen.

The doctor walked into the kitchen. He was young, couldn't have been more than thirty. After Raymond introduced Dr. Jean Proost to me, he pulled my identity out of the hat as he had sprung it earlier on the woman. The doctor looked surprised but not startled. He smiled warmly. He was very pleased to have me, he said. While the doctor ate his lunch, Raymond recounted the story, which by now I was hearing for the fourth or fifth time. But

I noted the pleasure with which they were receiving it, smiling and nodding, so I didn't mind hearing it again.

We talked about plans for my escape. At the outset the doctor said that it was dangerous for me to stay at their home because the house was also his office, and too many people walked in unexpectedly at all hours of the day and night. I would have to leave by five o'clock that afternoon.

So I pulled out the silk handkerchief from my escape kit, and we began to study the map. As we tried to make some sense out of the different roads over the border, I became increasingly apprehensive. There was no way of knowing from the map where the populated areas were, where the enemy checkpoints might be, what the terrain was like. As I asked some of these questions, not really expecting an answer, Raymond also sensed my concerns. He exchanged some words with his in-laws and then said to me that they had a cousin who lived about eleven kilometers from the French border. The cousin knew the border well, and Raymond was sure that he would help me get across. Raymond would give me the address.

Before I could even respond to this new idea, Raymond said, "No, Georges. You cannot go alone. I will go with you to our cousin."

This time I didn't even put up a pretense of protest. As the plan stood, Raymond and I would leave at five o'clock that afternoon for the relative's house. We would try to stay there overnight and all the next day. The following night I would take off for the border.

"Our cousin would know the best routes to take you across. But do you have somewhere to go when you get to France?" the doctor asked.

"No," I said. "When I get to France I will head for Paris. I will try to reach the people just as I did in Belgium. I have confidence that they will help me."

In reality, I was anything but confident. The thought of

crossing the border on my own and—assuming I made it—
traveling in France as a foreigner without any papers, without
anyone to contact, wasn't a very cheering prospect. I was still
hoping to connect with an escape organization, and would have
preferred to do so here in Belgium.

So I asked the doctor, "Aren't there people around who make
it their business to help fallen *aviateurs*?"

I avoided mention of the words "underground" or "organization"; I did not want to arouse suspicion that I might be a
German agent. But a doctor has patients and gets around.
Certainly, I thought, he must know someone who might have a
tie with the resistance.

"I don't know of anyone," he said. Then he was lost in
thought.

"Of course, there's the 'White Brigade,'" he offered hesi-
tantly, after a pause.

"Now you're cooking with gas," I thought. My pulse quickened. Maybe he could get to them? Maybe he was one of them
and was just being cautious before committing himself? "But
they are so *mysterieuse*," he added. "They are everywhere. But
no one knows who they are. I do not know how to find them. We
had better concentrate on the plan we have here."

What a terrible letdown! We went back to studying the map.
But I could see that the doctor was not concentrating on what we
were doing. He remained quiet while Raymond and I went on
discussing the plans for a while. Then he stood up abruptly and
said he had to go out to visit some patients.

It was raining cats and dogs outside, a cold November rain.
The urgency with which he decided to brave this inclement
weather made me feel that perhaps the seed I had planted had
taken effect. Confirming my thought, Dr. Proost repeated, "I'm
going to visit some patients. I will be back. Perhaps I will find
something."

We waited.

After cycling for about an hour in a freezing downpour, he returned, soaked to the bone. He looked satisfied, and I thought he must have met with success—but not quite. He had gone to the home of a fellow he knew who, he said, occasionally had given him an underground newspaper. The doctor thought this young man might know someone in the resistance who could help me. He was not home, but a message was left with the parents asking the young man to show up at the doctor's home no later than 5:00 P.M. If the man had not come by then, Raymond and I would leave for the border and carry out our original plan.

Now we really had to sweat out the rest of the afternoon. There was nothing to do but wait. The minutes ticked off slowly.

Five minutes to five arrived, and the man hadn't come. The doctor and his wife looked worried. Raymond looked worried. And I was worried. The prospect of crossing that border on my own and wandering in Nazi-occupied France looked more and more unappealing to me.

At five o'clock I got up to go. It was still pouring outside. Without saying a word the young woman walked out of the room and came back with a raincoat, which she told me to put on. I was deeply touched by this generosity and sacrifice, for I knew the coat could not be replaced for a long time. Raymond also put on his hat and coat. I said goodbye to the brave couple. Raymond and I headed for the door.

The doorbell rang.

My heart started pounding like a sledgehammer. Raymond and I scurried back into the room on the ground floor, while the doctor went to answer the door. I heard voices and someone being ushered upstairs to the doctor's office.

Raymond and I looked at each other, not daring to speak. They seemed to be taking a very long time up there. At last the doctor came down to call Raymond upstairs. A few minutes later Raymond rushed in, threw his arms around me, kissed me on both cheeks, and danced me off my feet.

"It's him, Georges! It's him. Now you are saved! I'm so happy."

He shook my hands and danced and laughed again.

"You see, I told you I would take care of you. Just leave it to me, I told you. You are saved now. In a few days you will be back in England. I told you I would save you. Didn't I tell you? But first you have to go upstairs and answer a few questions."

Upstairs in the office I was greeted by a tall, skinny young man. He smiled at me and seemed to be as excited and nervous as I was. He put me through a series of questions in broken English. After he had me recount the events of the previous day, about the mission and what happened in the field, he produced a folded piece of onionskin paper, a typed questionnaire in English.

Before I was through, I had to give my name, rank, and serial number; my father's name and my mother's maiden name; my birthplace, the birthplace of my mother, and my home address; the name of my squadron commander; and answers to other questions, seemingly irrelevant, including one on baseball. Then he added a description: height—5′ 10½″; complexion— fair; hair—blond; face—oval. This was information for my passport, he said. I thought it was for an added check on my identity.

"Now, you wait here. I'll be back by eight o'clock if everything is okay."

Some more waiting. It couldn't be helped. We had been briefed by our intelligence officers on the procedure: he had to go to the secret wireless and send a coded message to London, then wait for a reply, positive or negative. I realized he would also have to prepare a place for me to stay.

The next hours were spent under happier circumstances. The tension was largely gone, and all of us were relaxed. The doctor went out to make some real calls, and Hedwige was busy with household chores. Raymond and I played cards. He taught me whist and a new game, Chinese bridge. He trounced me every time. I showed him some of my stale card tricks, which used to go over big with kids under six. We laughed and joked and swapped stories and passed the time.

I became a little edgy as eight o'clock approached, but at eight and not a minute before, the young man reappeared. He said everything was all right, and he had some instructions for me.

"I will leave first to see if everything is clear. Then you will follow. Absolutely no talking. If you are stopped, remember, you do not know me. You never saw me before. I will pay your fare on the trolley. When we get inside, you will not talk to me or know me. Just watch when I get off and follow. For tonight, I am taking you to my house."

"I understand." I thought that an underground agent's home was not the safest place, but I figured he had not been able to set up another house in the little time he had.

"Goodbye, Raymond. Goodbye, Hedwige. Goodbye, Dr. Proost. I'll never, never forget you."

We walked out into a cold drizzle. And I was happy. I was on my way at last to my first station on this new "underground railway."

9

The War within the War

From here on my escape was no longer a stab in the dark, a hit-or-miss proposition. I no longer had any decisions to make. Everything was planned for me. The spontaneity was gone but not the hazards. The underground was well organized, but it was up against a well-oiled and ruthless machine. The greatest danger to me and my protectors came not from the Gestapo but from the homegrown Fascists known as the Black Brigades, who drew their cadres from the Vlaams Nationaal Verbond and the Walloon Rexists (monarchists) led by the Fascist Léon De Grelle. They were the eyes and ears of the Gestapo, and their agents were operating everywhere among the people.

I now entered a new world and a new war—the war within the war. It went on relentlessly, day in and day out, without letup. The Fascist use of terror, torture, concentration camps brought incalculable suffering and millions of casualties. The resistance countered with sabotage, guerrilla raids, partisan warfare, propaganda, and humor.

Yes, humor, believe it or not. The Belgians, like the Americans, are great practical jokers and pranksters. I was to learn much about this side of their character during my stay in Brussels.

It was early Saturday night, but the streets were deserted when the young man ushered me quickly into the ground floor of a two-story building at Tilmont Street 9, in the Jette district of Brussels. His parents welcomed me with pleasant smiles. Their names were Octave and Thérèse Malfait. The young man's name was Henri.

The Malfaits were a gentle couple who didn't fit any preconceived stereotype of the heroic resistance fighter. Octave Malfait was an accountant. He left early in the morning and returned in the early afternoon. Thérèse Malfait had to spend a good part of her day out foraging for scarce food and necessities. Young Henri Malfait was also out of the house most of the time. That left me and the older man together a lot. Malfait was not only congenial company; he was also well informed, and we talked about the conditions of life in occupied Belgium.

Every evening Octave Malfait would bring me the leading French language newspaper, *Le Soir* (the Evening). The Belgians called it *Le Soir Volé* (the stolen *Soir*) because it had been taken over by the Nazis and had become a craven propaganda sheet. It extolled the "new order" under Hitler and wrote glowingly of German victories and economic successes. It was laced with anti-Bolshevism and scurrilous anti-Semitism, which consumed me with revulsion and anger. Yet the Malfaits and I derived some perverse pleasure from reading its outlandish claims of victories when we knew that Hitler was losing the war.

As Armistice Day approached, I could sense an undercurrent of excitement in the Malfait family. This was the third Armistice Day since the occupation, and the Germans feared that any celebration of the Belgian national holiday might turn into a demonstration against the occupation. Consequently, they banned all observances of the day—a blow to the national pride of the Belgians, who were determined to retaliate and found several ways to do so.

One day Malfait came in with a leaflet issued by the Front de l'Independence, an umbrella organization of resistance groups. It promised an imminent British and American invasion from the north and the inevitable overthrow of Hitler. It called for heightened resistance to the Nazi occupation. Thousands of these leaflets appeared out of nowhere and were found on park benches, on streetcars, in factories, in lavatories, and other public places.

Then one afternoon, Octave Malfait came into the house and with great excitement told me the following story:

An armament depot was ordered to prepare a shipment of machine guns and ammunition for a certain German unit. A detail of German soldiers appeared with written orders, signed for it, loaded the stuff on their truck and drove away. Fifteen minutes later another truck appeared with papers requesting the same supplies. The supply officer explained that a detail had already been there and had taken the armaments back to their unit. The officer in charge of the second detail said there must be some mistake; no other section of his unit had orders to collect the guns and ammo. What the outcome of their argument was, no one knew, but every patriot in Belgium did know that the first detail on the scene had been a group of White Brigaders dressed in German uniforms, armed with the forged papers and a generous supply of guts.

Another day Malfait brought me the news that a Belgian flag was flying defiantly from the highest building in Brussels. It had been seen by many people, and the story was all over town, to the embarrassment and consternation of the Germans.

And on Tuesday, November 9, when he came home later than usual, Octave spread *Le Soir* before me on the dining room table and watched my face expectantly. I scanned the front page. The masthead, the format, the headlines—everything looked as usual. Suddenly, I did a double-take. In the upper left-hand corner a two-column photograph of a Flying Fortress on a bomb run jumped right out of the page. In the lower opposite corner was a photo of a mournful Hitler, his head tilted upward, his arms crossed over his chest, exclaiming, *"Dass Habe Ich . . ."* (this I have).

My pleasure and excitement soared as I began to read under

neutral headings—"Anniversary," "A Document," "News from the Countryside"—stories about Russian, British, and American victories and the coming Allied invasion of Europe from across the English Channel. There were items about the successes of the resistance. And mostly the pages were filled with humor and biting satire that poked fun at the Germans and their collaborators, the Black Brigades.

The Malfaits and I laughed for hours at the cartoons and articles as we read them over and over. Octave told me that this lampoon edition had arrived at the kiosks before the normal edition of the paper was delivered. Word had spread like wildfire throughout Brussels, and very soon long queues were forming at the newsstands. The printed price on the masthead was sixty centimes, but people were paying ten francs and more. Later, when it was sold out, copies went for huge sums on the black market.

Unbelievable! For one glorious, exhilarating moment the resistance had stolen back the stolen *Le Soir.*

How did they do it? A full-sized newspaper could not be put out on a closet mimeograph. It required a large press with skilled compositors and pressmen, knowledge of all the distribution points, and a network large enough to bundle and distribute thousands of papers. With so many involved, security had to be tight. And the timing had to be perfect to reach the kiosks just a few minutes before the normal edition.

The scheme had to be a master stroke of organizational genius. Was it worth the risk? Undoubtedly the Belgian resistance thought so. And judging from its impact on the Malfait family, I could see that it was well worth it. The thousands who received the paper plus the thousands more to whom it was passed on plus the additional thousands who heard about it added up to deal a damaging blow to the myth of the invincibility of the German "superman." I desperately wanted to keep a copy and smuggle it out with me, but the rules were strict. I was not permitted to take anything out.

All was not fun and games by any means. The life of the Belgians was characterized more by a grim struggle to survive. Food was scarce and strictly rationed. A flourishing black market really benefited only the better-off, yet the average Belgian had to purchase necessities on the black market to keep from starving, saving and scraping from meager earnings to be able to do so.

One day Malfait came back from the street and said, "Look at this." There was anger in his voice as he handed me an American dollar bill. That is, at first glance it looked like a dollar bill. But it wasn't. It was a darn good facsimile, and Malfait told me that they were being grabbed up in the street as if they were the real thing.

"Open it," said Octave.

The dollar opened up like a butterfly. Across the centerfold inside was a yellow Star of David. The legend read: "This dollar has no value without the Jew Morganthau's signature. This dollar pays for the Jewish war. This dollar has no smell, but the Jew has one."

I was gratified to see that Malfait was angry. I hadn't told him that I was Jewish; I knew that the penalty for harboring a Jew was even greater than for harboring an American flyer. Why place an additional burden on the family?

I folded the "bill" and hid it in the heel of my right shoe. Yes, I disobeyed the rules.

During these days I saw very little of Henri Malfait. He was a scout leader and a member of the Catholic Youth Movement; he was enrolled at the university but didn't spend very much time studying. He was usually out of the house doing things for the resistance.

For one thing, he was involved in the distribution of *La Libre*

Belgique, an illegal newspaper. "My father got me started on this," he told me. "He used to get one copy from a friend at work, and I helped him make additional copies in longhand to put in the mailboxes of friends and neighbors. Then my father bought an old typewriter, so old it had separate keys for capital letters. But now we have some help, and we get out about thirty to fifty copies."

Henri also did some intelligence work. "One day I was sent to a big industrial area outside Brussels to find out where the Germans repaired and rebuilt aircraft motors. I was inside a factory when a guard came up to me. 'What are you doing here?' I had to think fast. 'I'm looking for the exit. Where is the exit?'' I was so convincing that the German told me the way to a certain exit. To get there I had to walk through the entire factory. I saw everything. I was better informed," Henri said, laughing.

I knew Henri was involved in other activities, but he was careful not to reveal too much, and I didn't ask questions. I was fully aware of the danger of too much knowledge if I were captured; I was also aware of the danger of arousing suspicion of being a German spy. Even though I had passed the first screening, the questionnaire, and the physical description radioed to London, I could still have been a Nazi spy attempting to penetrate the underground apparatus. We had been briefed on how such a scheme worked. The Germans would recondition an American or British plane that had been forced down in Europe. They would send it aloft at the time of a raid, and a Gestapo agent would bail out. He would go up to some farmhouse, claim to be an American or British flyer, and ask for help in escaping the Germans. He would have an assumed identity, dogtags, and a physical resemblance to a missing flyer, enough to pass the first screening. He would speak English with an American or British accent, as called for, and pass into the underground network. He would ride this "underground railway" all the way to Paris and then disappear. At the precise moment of his disappearance, every one connected with his escape would be rounded up by the Gestapo.

I knew from our briefings that such things had happened, and I was sure Henri knew of them from his experience. As if to drive the point home, Henri had told me on November 7 or 8 that they had discovered a German spy trying to penetrate the organization. Someone was going to give him the questionnaire and then arrange to have him shot. I didn't ask how they knew he was a spy, and I continued to be careful not to ask too many questions about resistance activities.

But though Henri and I did not discuss the organization, we did discuss the politics of the resistance. I remember his telling me that 90 percent of the Belgian people opposed the occupation. There was an intense hatred of the Germans—understandable among a people twice invaded in less than a quarter-century. But the feeling wasn't merely anti-German; it was also anti-Fascist, for the Belgians were experiencing at firsthand not just the wartime atrocities, real or imagined, that occurred in World War I but a ruthless, totally barbaric effort to destroy their identity and spirit as a people.

Henri was an idealist with strong religious beliefs. An anti-Fascist in his convictions, he said he shared these beliefs with a large number of Catholic youth under the official blessing of the Church. How different from my experience in Spain, where even though the majority of Catholics supported the Loyalist government, the official Church was with the Fascists.

While I knew that many disparate groups were part of the resistance, my own experience and affiliation with the Communist left had conditioned me to see the Communists and Socialists as the major force in the underground, and to downplay the role of the Catholics and others. My firsthand experience with Henri and the Malfaits was an eyeopener. It extended my horizons and compelled me to arrive at a more balanced view of the anti-Hitler movement.

Part of me today looks back with nostalgia to that feeling of camaraderie which united people of different ideologies in a struggle against a common foe. This may very well be a naive perception, for undoubtedly there were deep differences and rivalries, organizational jockeying for position and power. But these were largely held in check by the common objective of defeating German and Italian Fascism.

Even so, the seeds of future division were revealed in a conversation I had with Henri's older brother Leon, who showed up at the Malfait house on the third or fourth day of my stay. Leon was a worker priest employed in a large locomotive repair works. In response to my questions he told me about the intolerable working conditions, the long hours, the low wages. He talked about the Belgians' hatred of the Germans and said there was a deliberate slowdown by the workers.

Then he said very quietly, as if talking to himself, "I am afraid the workers are a little too far to the left. After the war I am afraid they will bring in socialism."

While this was a troubling thought to Leon, to me it was just the reverse. I was pleased to hear it.

"Perhaps, if that is what the workers want, it would be all right," I said in an equally quiet tone. "Why do you fear socialism?"

"It might turn the workers against the Church," he replied.

I tried to reassure him, saying that I thought socialism would not necessarily turn the workers against their Catholicism. Their attitude would probably depend on whether the Church opposed social change that the workers wanted.

I don't think I assuaged his fears, nor did either of us change our views. But I felt a closeness and affection for Leon and all the Malfaits that I cherish to this day.

On Thursday, November 11, Henri told me I would be leaving

the Malfaits. There wasn't much advance notice; that night, Jacques De Bruyn, a tall man with blond hair, came to take me to dinner at his mother's home, and after dinner Madame De Bruyn escorted me on the tram all the way across Brussels to a new safe house.

10

All That Glitters

A man about forty years old, of medium height and with reddish hair, met me at the door of his second-floor apartment and asked me to remove my shoes. He handed me a pair of house slippers and walked me to the kitchen, where he put my shoes in a compartment of the huge Belgian stove. This was my introduction to the Thibaut family.

Raoul Thibaut was an electrical engineer. His wife stayed home with their infant daughter. They had a keen interest in everything that was going on. They asked informed questions about America and about the lives of the American people. They admired Roosevelt and were curious about the New Deal and American politics. We spent hours discussing the Russians, the British, the Germans.

I had only one complaint against Raoul Thibaut: while I wanted to improve my French, he wanted to practice his English and insisted that we speak English only. I yielded to my host, naturally.

With Madame Thibaut it was different. While she understood English and was able to be part of the conversation at the table, I remember her speaking French to me. She was a dynamic person who talked with great passion and conviction about everything. She spoke rapidly, and it was hard for me to follow her. I often had to ask her to slow down. Still, I was getting the practice I wanted. As passionate as she was in her convictions about the evils of German Fascism, she was equally involved and devoted to her infant daughter, Inès. I, too, became attached to the baby and spent delightful hours playing with her.

On a couple of occasions friends came to dinner. We engaged in the usual discussions that went on in any middle-class family anywhere in the world. It was hard to remember that outside, a dangerous enemy was waging a cruel and deadly war. It was hard to remember that the father who went off to work every day and the mother who stayed home caring for an eighteen-month-old girl could be seasoned combatants in this war within the war.

Apart from Henri, these were the first underground pros I had met. They had consciously joined a movement, had committed themselves to fight to the end, and knew the consequences of their commitment. I was not the first nor, I assumed, the last Allied flyer to be helped by them.

On the fifth day of my stay in their apartment at 134 Avenue du Diamant, Raoul came home early from work and said, "George, we're going out."

"Isn't it dangerous?"

"It's no good for anyone to be cooped up so long," he said.

"Well, all right, if you say so." I knew we were breaking the rules. I was excited and not a little nervous.

We took the tram downtown. It was early afternoon; the car was crowded, and we had to stand. Raoul and I stood side by side. We did not observe the underground rule about keeping a distance between us. As we left the tram, Raoul drew my attention to the *Defense de Fumer* (No Smoking) signs on the tram. I wondered why he did so but could ask nothing at the time. In fact, I didn't talk at all on the trip. And Raoul spoke only in French, in case we might be overheard.

We strolled down a busy avenue. I was amazed at the liveliness, the hustle and bustle of downtown Brussels. The shop windows were stocked with rich displays of goods. It was still a little over a month till Christmas, yet there was a decidedly holiday atmosphere. Toys and clothes were abundantly and lavishly displayed. People stopped in front of the windows to admire electric trains and dolls.

Unbelievable! Is this occupied Europe? Where did they get the goods in the midst of such an all-encompassing war? Where were the shortages that the Belgians had complained to me about? Was this the real Belgium? I couldn't ask Raoul. I had to wait for answers until we returned home.

On Avenue Louis we passed an imposing, official-looking building. Raoul told me it was the central Gestapo headquarters. Every day since the beginning of the occupation, three Belgian patriots had been executed there—a grim reminder of the true Brussels under the Nazis.

Raoul acted the gracious host and tour guide. "Would you like some refreshment?"

I nodded assent. He took me to a large, attractive restaurant with enormous mirrors that made the place look even bigger than it was. On a raised platform in one corner of the huge dining room a small group of musicians played Viennese waltzes. The atmosphere was festive. It felt like Vienna. Raoul ordered coffee and buns, and we sat there quietly watching the comings and goings of very decently dressed men and women.

We left the restaurant and queued up for a movie. Inside the dark movie theater I felt especially safe. I enjoyed the picture, even though I could barely follow the French dialogue (inconsiderately, they had neglected to provide the English subtitles).

Back at the house, I asked the Thibauts how they accounted for the contradictions I had seen that day. Every place I'd been in Belgium, I was told of meager food rations and short supplies of clothing and durable goods. Yet in downtown Brussels there were lighted shop windows displaying costly wares, cinemas with long queues, crowded restaurants with musicians, pastry and bonbon shops, department stores offering trick toys and electric trains, a holiday atmosphere. None of this jibed with everything I thought I had learned about the condition of a country under three years of occupation.

"All is not gold that glitters," Raoul replied. The Germans maintained a few cities in occupied Europe, notably Paris and Brussels, as show places where German officers and war profiteers could take their wives and mistresses to show them a good time and buy them gifts. But there was a vast difference between the outside of the shops and the inside, he explained. Inside, though the prewar trimmings remained lavish, there was very little on the shelves. And the little that was there was beyond the reach of the average Belgian. Only German officers and the collaborators who were doing business with them had enough money to purchase those few luxuries; it was hard enough for the others to keep up with the actual necessities of life.

The ordinary Belgian was constantly on the edge of starvation. Life was a little better in the country villages, where—despite requisitioning of food—farmers were able to hide some produce, much of which found its way into the black market. The rations were so slim that practically everyone had to patronize the black market. I remember Leon Malfait asking me with some disbelief, "In America, George, you do not purchase from the black market?"

"Yes, there is a black market in America. But people do not have to use it to keep from starving. And it is thought unpatriotic to use it." I must have sounded very virtuous.

Raoul asked me if I had noticed the No Smoking signs on the tram. I said yes, but in New York, subways and streetcars always had No Smoking signs. What was so significant about these?

"In Brussels, we never had them," he said. "They were introduced only recently." He explained why by telling me this story:

One day a German officer emerged from a crowded tram and made his way peacefully to his quarters. But when he removed his coat, he noticed something peculiar: all over the back were little holes—unmistakably the marks of cigarette burns. How did they get there? Someone was going too far with practical jokes—but who? Where had he been? Had he taken off his jacket anywhere?

Then he remembered the crowded tram. That was the only place it could have happened. "The Belgian swine! Those bastards! They will pay for this." The officer grabbed his coat and started for the door. But suddenly he stopped in his tracks. "Hold on. I can't do this. I'd be the laughingstock of all the officers. Imagine some Belgian swine outwitting an officer of the Third Reich!" So he put on another coat and got rid of the damaged one.

But the real damage was already done. In many Belgian homes one member of the family was telling and retelling the story of a practical joke played by an intrepid Belgian on a German officer that evening on the crowded tram. The story spread, and in a few days it became impossible for a German soldier to ride the tram during rush hour without having his tunic riddled with cigarette holes.

And that is why there are No Smoking signs on the trams of Brussels!

My stay with the Thibauts was pleasant enough, but I was becoming increasingly worried about my wife and family back home. I knew they wouldn't get word of my safety until I returned to England. I thought of the dangers I still had to face on the long road ahead, and I was anxious to be on my way.

So when Madame De Bruyn came to the house on the eighth day of my stay and told me that I would be moving out that night, I was very much relieved. She told me that she would take me, with another escapee, to the French border by rail. There we would cross into France on foot in order to avoid Nazi checkpoints. The rules would be very strict as before. She would be several paces in front of us, but we were not to speak to her or to each other.

That evening as I kissed the baby and the Thibauts goodbye, I was beginning to have that queasy feeling in the pit of my stomach again.

It was soon gone as the excitement of the night's adventure took over.

11

I Meet the French Resistance

It was dark when the other escapee and I followed Madame De Bruyn aboard the train. The ride from Brussels to the French border took about an hour. We got off at Rumes and followed our guide to the end of the station platform. We stepped into a shadow behind a large structure. She told us to wait there while she disappeared into the blackness. She returned shortly with several men and women.

I could hear muffled voices but could not see faces. Suddenly, through the whispers, I caught a high-pitched southern drawl.

"Johnson!" I was about to yell but controlled myself. I stepped forward and whispered, "Hi, Johnson." He was startled—but then we had ourselves one great reunion. From that moment on, H.C. "Tennessee" Johnson, our flight engineer, and I traveled together.

We were now four escapees with a woman and a man as guides. After hiking for an hour through woods, up and down hills, we came to a large farmhouse. The guides went in first, then beckoned us to follow.

Inside the large kitchen there were five or six people—one woman, three or four men and a twelve-year-old boy.

"Welcome to Free France!" they said. "You are now in the hands of the French resistance." They slapped us on the back, congratulated us, and expressed their admiration. Food and wine appeared. They toasted us, and we toasted them. We drank to the death of Hitler. We laughed and ate, and the wine flowed freely. We got pleasantly high.

The boy was wide-eyed with hero worship. Like any kid back home, he was in awe of flyers and airplanes. He plied us with questions about bombers, about fighter planes, about air battles. He asked us to compare the Spitfires and Mustangs against the Messerschmidts and Focke-Wulfs; he wanted to know how many enemy fighters we had shot down—and on and on.

I was just as excited about the boy as he was about us. We talked about the French resistance. He said he was an active member and boasted about his exploits. I could not get over the courage of the boy. He was twelve years old, doing a job dangerous even for an adult.

For Johnson and me the stop was our first opportunity to exchange stories. He had found Harrenstein, the radio operator, and Craig, the tail gunner, badly shot up and lying motionless on the floor of the radio compartment; they were dead. After I had crawled to the tail and brought Craig back to life, just minutes later he was dead. How tragically ironic. He was only nineteen, the youngest member of our crew. Bramwell, the pilot, though wounded, had desperately held on to the controls to pull the plane out of its dive, allowing the crew time to bail out.

I now had the answer to a question that had bothered me. I had counted seven chutes in the air that day, but I couldn't remember whether it was seven with or without mine. Now that I knew two men were dead, it had to be eight parachutes. Since I had been told that five of our crew were captured, there had to be another escapee. Johnson and I wondered who it might be; it would be weeks before we knew it was John Maiorca.

Tennessee was slightly wounded. But being the luckiest son of a gun I knew—well, maybe next to me, when it comes to escape and survival—he'd landed right near a farmhouse. An old lady took him to a barn and told him to hide in the hay and wait. She came back that evening, took him to her home and fed him. A man came by, asked him if he had a gun, and went away disappointed when he was told no. He exchanged his flying clothes for a pair of trousers, a shirt, a coat, shoes and socks, taking care to tear off all his name labels from his military gear. From there on his journey was arranged. That night he cycled with an underground agent to a house some distance away. "That's all there was to it," he said.

Early next morning the twelve-year-old boy had the chance to demonstrate his courage. He was one of the guides who took us cross-country to the railroad station inside the French border. There we picked up another guide, who rode with us all the way to Paris.

As the train raced through the rolling French countryside, I kept thinking about the last time I had seen Paris. It was in January 1939. Dr. Juan Negrín, prime minister of the Spanish Republican government, in a last-ditch effort to force a withdrawal of the German and Italian troops in Spain, had ordered the unilateral withdrawal of all International Brigades fighting on the Loyalist side, and the main body of Lincoln Brigaders had been repatriated in time for Christmas. (Abraham Lincoln Brigade was the term used in the United States to describe all American volunteers in Spain. The Lincoln Battalion was an infantry unit of the XVth International Brigade.) But I came down with typhoid fever and was sent to the army hospital at Vich.

I was completely out of it with a high fever for ten days; then I watched as another body was wheeled out of the typhoid ward each day and wondered when my turn would come. And that was not my only worry. The hospital lay directly in the path of Franco's advancing armies, and despite the hospital markings we were bombed repeatedly by German Stukas and Italian Savoias. As the Loyalist armies kept retreating, the wounded were evacuated from hospital to hospital until we arrived at Mataro on the Mediterranean.

Weak from the fever and badly underweight, I was given double rations of rice to fatten me up. I was soon well enough to travel to Ripoll in northern Catalonia, where I caught up with a group of Americans leaving Spain. Ours turned out to be the last Loyalist train to cross the Pyrenees into France. It was a close call, for the very next day, January 26, Barcelona fell to the Fascists, and defeated Republican refugees in the tens of thousands had to cross the treacherous snow-covered mountains on foot.

We had traveled to Le Havre in sealed cars under the auspices of the League of Nations. When we got to Paris, the French government sealed off the station as well. No one was permitted to leave or enter. But our spirits soared as a crowd of Parisians waiting for us outside the closed gate burst into the stirring strains of the "Marseillaise." We raised clenched fists in the Popular Front salute and sang lustily along with them. Nevertheless, the last time I saw Paris, I didn't see Paris.

This time, at the Gare du Nord, Johnson and I were turned over to a woman dressed in black. Our guide walked, or rather ambled ahead of us. She seemed to be wandering aimlessly down the street, stopping every now and then in front of a shop window and glancing furtively back in our direction. She led us to the Metro and eventually to an area of large apartment houses, where we ducked into one of the buildings and climbed up five or six flights to an apartment on the top floor.

To my surprise, I found the place crawling with people. There were at least four or five Allied flyers in addition to Johnson and me and the two others who had been on our train. There were also family members and the two guides. I thought it was dangerous and crazy to have so many of us in one apartment.

Crazy or not, we had a great evening swapping combat and escape stories. Some were real thrillers. One or two of the men had been captured by the Germans and managed to break away. Another had landed in Germany and literally walked out. A

Spitfire pilot of the Polish RAF, a contingent of the British Air Force, had been wounded and had made a forced landing in Belgium or France. He got away from his plane before the Germans got to him.

We talked about our exploits. I remember that Harold Pope was there, a stocky flight engineer of the 100th, our sister bomb group. On the Schweinfurt raid both his pilot and copilot had been killed and the plane severely damaged. Though he had no more than the usual six hours of "stick time" that all of us gunners had been given in training, he took over the controls of his B-17 and brought her in for a safe landing. He had won a well-deserved citation for that extraordinary feat.

Naturally, we fought over the relative merits of our planes. The Liberator (B-24) men claimed that their ships were safer because their tapered wing gave them more speed. We Flying Fortress (B-17) men argued that our ships were safer because the wide wing allowed the plane to pull out of a dive, giving us time to bail out; the B-24s were flying coffins, we declared. And the RAF guys said we both were crazy to fly daylight missions because the casualties were heavier. And we said true, but we would never want to fly nights and face the dread of midair collisions. And so it went, well into the night.

The next day we were split up. Johnson and I were taken to a new hideout in Vanves, a suburb of Paris. The house was a large rambling structure in a yard surrounded by a wall eight feet high. There was a huge dining room with large French doors opening into a yard with trees and shrubs. In one wing of the house was a long corridor with a row of bedrooms on each side. It had a distinctly institutional look, and we soon found out why. Our host told us it was a former mental hospital, founded and operated by his father, who was now deceased.

Johnson and I slept in single beds in one of the bedrooms on this corridor. The family slept in the other wing of the house. There was the father, who was a doctor, his wife, and a grown daughter. All three left the house every day, the doctor to his clinic, the wife to some activity, and the daughter to work. There was a middle-aged cook and a young servant who cleaned, made the beds, and served the meals.

The house was large and spacious. Since we were protected by the wall, we didn't have to draw the blinds and so didn't feel cooped up. But despite the comfortable surroundings and apparent affluence of the family, they still shared the wartime hardships of the French people. There was no coal or wood. The only heat in the entire house came from a small round stove in the dining room that burned sawdust. And it was lit only twice a day, providing heat—over no more than a two- or three-foot radius—that lasted about two hours after each lighting.

The igniting procedure took place in the morning and again at four o'clock in the afternoon. The hostess or the servant would stand a round piece of wood, which looked like an untapered baseball bat, in the center of the stove. She would fill the stove with sawdust and pack it down, then remove the bat and light the sawdust at the bottom of the tubular hole it left. The fuel would burn very slowly up the center, throwing off its pitifully small amount of heat.

Our solicitous hosts insisted that Johnson and I stay in bed till late in the morning to give the stove time to warm up. So we missed the morning lighting show. When we got out of bed, we would sit down within a foot or two of the stove to warm our hands and feet before going to the table for breakfast. But we never warmed up. It was so cold even in bed that Johnson and I took to sleeping close together in a single bed, sandwiched between our two mattresses, to conserve our body heat. Still, we never felt really warm.

Food was likewise scarce. There was much less than we had found in Belgium. Our main staples were potatoes, bread, small quantities of vegetables, and very little meat or fowl. For dessert there were apples and cheese. It was during my stay in Vanves that I learned to appreciate what marvelous cooks the French were, however little they had to work with. Potatoes were the main dish every night, yet those potatoes were never prepared the same way twice. They were dished up with different vegetables and herbs, and each meal was served elegantly. Nevertheless, we were hungry all the time.

I felt guilty about sharing the family's meager rations and tried to refrain from reaching for the small second helpings that were left temptingly before us on the table. But my hollow cheeks gave me a cadaverous look that aroused the motherly sympathy of the cook and our hosts, who kept urging me to eat. They said I must gain strength for the ordeal still ahead. I resisted. They kept insisting. So I took the second helping, but never without some feelings of guilt.

We settled down for a long stay. We had no idea how long, but we knew from our guide that there was trouble. The day after we arrived in Paris, the Gestapo had penetrated an entire chain in the underground. Many people were arrested, and the line was broken. The resistance needed time to repair the network and bring reserves and new hiding places into the service.

For us, the escapees, it was an inconvenience; it delayed our departure from Paris and increased the danger. But for the resistance fighters who were arrested, it was the ultimate tragedy. I knew they faced imprisonment, torture, and possible execution. I did not personally know these people, but I could not help thinking of the Malfaits, the Thibauts, and the beautiful people in Zele and Hamme—and the possibility that they too could pay this price.

Aside from struggling to keep warm and trying to keep our minds off our hunger, we spent countless hours reading, talking, playing solitaire and poker. The stakes—all on paper—were high, and we kept careful records of winnings and losses. Johnson, as I've already mentioned, was the luckiest gambler, whether it was shooting craps, playing cards, or tossing a coin for the flight engineer position on our crew and leaving me to settle for assistant flight engineer. So it was no surprise that I ended up owing him about half a million dollars. (I confess that I welshed on the debt.)

Tennessee Johnson had a wonderful sense of humor as well and was a great storyteller—a great tall-story teller, I should say—with a gift for the colorful metaphor: "It rained like a cow pissin' on a flat rock," he'd say. But even H.C.'s stories ran out of steam. And reading in French was getting tiresome, and I was getting bored with losing so much money at poker.

I had too much time to worry about the family at home. "Missing in Action," as frightening as such an announcement is for the family, is still better than "Killed in Action," but the uncertainty adds a terrible strain. The longer my stay here, the longer their suffering. I knew that Margie was not just sitting and waiting. Soon after I had left for the army, she had traded in her master's degree in social work and a good position with a family agency for a job in an aircraft plant on Long Island. After a hard day's work as a riveter on airplane tail sections, she still had to care for young Danny when she got home.

Margie had been Danny's mother since he was sixteen months old. I knew she loved him just as if he were her biological son, perhaps more. And I knew she loved me. But I was feeling some pangs of guilt at having thrust this additional responsibility on her. In the Army Air Corps I had been trained as an airplane mechanic and could have discharged my wartime duties honorably without going into the wild blue yonder. At the time I volunteered to fly, the average life of an aerial gunner in combat was fifty seconds, according to the stories making the rounds. Did I have to do it?

All of this was on my mind as time dragged on. We had not been prepared by our intelligence briefings for such a long stay in Paris. We'd been told it was usually a one- or two-day stopover. Now we were here for God knew how long. The waiting became increasingly unbearable, and an old soldier's song we had learned from the British Battalion in Spain kept running through my mind:

> Waiting, waiting, waiting,
> always fucking well waiting,
> waiting in the morning,
> waiting in the night.
>
> God send the day
> when we'll fucking well
> wait no more.

The one break in the monotony was a most unwelcome one. Thanksgiving Day was dark and gloomy, and H.C. and I were busy torturing each other with the most detailed descriptions of the Thanksgiving dinner we were missing when we were startled by the loud piercing whine of an air raid siren. It penetrated the protective walls of our asylum and once again brought the war home to us. Ear-shattering blasts of antiaircraft opened up, sounding right next door. And then, sure enough, we heard the drone of heavy bombers. Johnson and I guessed they were Forts.

What a feeling! I had been in air raids in Spain many times. For us infantrymen it was air bombardment that scared us the most, even though artillery caused more casualties. And being bombed in a city could be even more frightening than at the front, as I found when I was on leave in Barcelona and Valencia.

But this was Johnson's first time on the receiving end of a raid. And besides—here was a new twist: it was our own side that was dropping the bombs on us. Was this poetic justice? Were we being given a taste of our own medicine? We wondered if our own 388th Bomb Group was involved. If so, this had to be the cruelest cut of all.

As it turned out, we didn't hear any bombs drop. The noise of the planes died away, the all-clear sounded, and Johnson and I went back to commiserating with each other.

At the end of about three weeks a courier came and took us back to Paris. I don't remember where we stayed. But I do remember a guide taking me out to a "photomaton" where I had my pictures taken. He kept two and gave me one, which I hid in my shoe along with the phony dollar bill I'd smuggled out of Belgium.

I also remember riding the Metro. At one of the transfer points two young boys were horsing around as they raced to catch a train. They looked like any two adolescents I'd seen anywhere, but I remember them vividly. On each one's chest was a yellow Star of David. This hit me even harder than the phony dollar.

That night, the courier returned with my forged identity. It was a letter of employment stating that I was being transferred as a *clerc* to a town in southern France. I was given a French name, and my picture was sealed in the upper left-hand corner of the letter.

Johnson and I were momentarily separated, and I remember his meeting our original female guide on the bank of the Seine, with me a safe distance away. The rendezvous was made to look like a lovers' tryst, and it was indeed a very romantic setting. But we didn't tarry long. We were soon aboard the night train to Bordeaux. Johnson and I were joined by a new guide and two escapees, a Scotsman and the Polish RAF pilot we'd met the night we arrived.

We were leaving Paris, and once again I didn't really get to see Paris. Well, strike that. Perhaps I had seen enough.

12

The Gestapo Looks Me Over

The train was already crowded when we boarded, and there were no seats left. So the four of us and our guide took up positions in the corridors of two adjoining cars, making sure to keep at least one other companion within view.

It was an overnight ride to Bordeaux, and I didn't relish the prospect of standing up all the way, but that was the least of my worries. In Paris we had been told by our courier that the train would stop at a checkpoint just before we arrived in Bordeaux. There, Gestapo officers would board the train and inspect the identification papers of all the passengers. There was no way around it. We just prayed that they wouldn't ask any questions, that's all. If they questioned us we were sunk. We could never pass as Frenchmen.

On the first leg of the trip I managed to sit down on the floor of the passageway and catch some sleep. But as morning approached, more and more passengers came aboard, and I had to stand up the rest of the way in a corridor jampacked like a New York subway crush. I couldn't sleep; I couldn't read; I couldn't talk, so I had plenty of time to think and worry about my forthcoming encounter with the Nazi inspectors.

Daylight came, and I was able to distract myself a little with the beautiful French countryside. The peaceful, imperturbable landscape was in sharp contrast to the anxieties and fears churning inside of me.

Just outside Bordeaux the train came to a halt in a wide clearing. Through the window I saw a cluster of German officers, standing on the ground below. They split up in pairs and boarded the train at several different points.

One pair boarded at the opposite end of the car behind me, and I watched with mounting nervousness as they examined papers, occasionally asking questions, working their way slowly through a mass of flesh toward my car. Then the rear door of my car opened, and I stood face to face with the enemy. He was a short mousy guy wearing high polished boots and a peaked officer's cap that made him look tall and forbidding.

"*Identités. S'il vous plait.*"

I handed him the letter. He took his sweet time reading it as I anxiously watched his face. He studied the photo. He looked up at me. I looked straight into his eyes. I was quaking with fear inside. He looked down at the picture again, then glanced up at me once more. He looked down at the letter a third time. My stomach dropped. I was bracing myself for the question.

"*Merci.*" That's all he said. He handed the letter back to me and turned to the next passenger.

I felt no joy, no exhilaration, nothing like the feeling I had that first time back in Hamme when the old man and I walked past the German soldiers. This time I was completely drained; I felt only relief. But the ordeal was over.

I don't remember now whether we changed trains in Bordeaux. But we did go on to Dax, where we got off, and our guide led us down the street around the back of a big shed. There a new guide was waiting for us with five bicycles. We each took one.

"Follow me," the guide said, unceremoniously mounting his bike and pedaling rapidly down the narrow street. He never even asked us if we knew how to ride before leading us through back ways and country lanes at a very fast clip. After about an hour's cycling, he swung off the road into some protective cover. There we lunched on bread, cheese, and wine and rested for about half an hour. He told us that we would travel faster on the next lap.

He was true to his word, and I found myself really struggling.

The countryside was exquisitely beautiful, but I could not enjoy it. The riding was sheer torture. My muscles had tightened up, and I developed a severe "charley horse." I began lagging behind the others. At one stop the guide told me I was slowing up the group and would have to pedal faster. At the advanced age of thirty, I was the old man of the group. What could I do? Of course I kept up. But I remained "tail-end Charley," as we said in the air force, throughout the entire trip.

Generally, we stayed on back lanes, avoiding populated areas, though I do remember at least once passing through a small village. The people looked at us but without curiosity. Men wearing berets and riding bikes are, I suppose, not an uncommon sight in southern France.

In the early evening we reached a main highway where the going was smoother, but we were now in hillier country, and the uphill stretches gave me considerable trouble. Fortunately, we had only a short distance to go before we stopped at an isolated house right on the road. At the back of this two-story house we were welcomed by a man and a woman, who quickly hid our bikes and brought us through the back door into a large chamber. Tables and chairs were set up for dining and drinking, and I could see that we were in a country inn.

Our hosts rushed us upstairs. The Pole and the Scotsman were put in one room; Johnson and I shared another. We washed up and rested on the beds till the woman brought us some food and wine. I was aching all over and thoroughly exhausted. I wanted nothing better than to get a good night's sleep. I was just beginning to doze off when we heard a commotion outside. I went to the window and cautiously peeked out. German soldiers were getting out of a car and heading for the inn, and soon a second carload arrived.

I knew, of course, that they had not come looking for us; they had come to eat and drink at the inn. Nevertheless, those German voices below us were unsettling, to say the least. We didn't dare talk or move or go to the toilet for fear they might hear us. As the evening wore on, their voices grew louder and they became boisterous. It wasn't easy falling asleep to that kind of music, but eventually fatigue got the better of me. At dawn, when we were awakened, the innkeeper told us that the Germans had been there till two o'clock.

After breakfast we mounted our bikes, and the ordeal started all over. Again we took to the back roads, and the terrain was getting more hilly now. We were in the foothills of the Pyrenees. A couple of hours later we stopped at a farmhouse, left our bikes, and started to climb a mountain.

I was relieved that the cycling was over, but now we were crossing the Pyrenees into Spain, and I knew what was in store for us. This was my second time to climb those treacherous mountains. Six years earlier, in August 1937, the French government had sealed off the border to keep military supplies and volunteers from getting into Spain. To reach the fighting, we had had to scale the Pyrenees at night, crossing the frontier before daybreak in order to elude the French border patrols.

I was not quite twenty-four then, and in good physical condition, but like most of the others I had had no experience climbing mountains and was not prepared for the ordeal. The ancient smugglers' trails along which we trudged single file were steep and rocky—and never ending: every time we reached a summit, thinking it was the last, there rose another hill above us. We tackled that one, and there was another, on and on. And as if that weren't enough to test our fortitude, we found, even after we reached the safety of Spain, that the descent had its own brand of torture. We kept stumbling and tripping, jarring our spines as we let ourselves down the rocky incline.

So now I anticipated the worst—and I was right. I swore afterward that I would never climb the Pyrenees again. Twice was enough!

This time it took longer. Instead of racing against the dawn in one night, we spent four days and three nights, hiking by day and resting in shelters at night. But this was mid-December, not August, and the thin coat I was wearing was no protection against those strong blustery winds blowing right through me. The old paper-thin shoes that Eduard Lauwaert had given me in Hamme were disintegrating. When the sole of my left shoe tore loose, I tied it on with a handkerchief. But snow caked inside, and I kept tripping over it. I tore the dangling sole off the shoe and walked the rest of the way with nothing between the snow and my wet stockinged foot. Why I didn't get frostbite, I still don't know.

We slept and ate in isolated farmhouses along the way. I remember spending one night in a barn next to some sheep, a goat, and a burro. All night long the snorting and farting of the animals and their pungent smells kept me awake. But at least their body heat kept us from freezing.

On the third day our guide left us, saying he was going down to town to make a phone call. He was gone all day. When nightfall came and he hadn't come back, we became a little anxious. We were still not out of danger. For Spain, though technically neutral in World War II, was a Fascist country, and Franco owed his victory over the Republican government to the massive aid he had received from Hitler and Mussolini. If the Guardia Mobile, the most notoriously Fascist and ruthless of the Spanish government forces, caught us in the mountains, there was a good chance they would turn us over to the German border patrols.

Furthermore, we had been cautioned in our intelligence briefings about a peculiar quirk in international law: the legal distinction between "escapee" and "evadee." If you had been captured by the enemy and managed to escape, you were an "escapee." If you had never been apprehended, you were an "evadee." The Franco government was obliged to return all escapees to their own governments, but evadees could be interned in Spain for the duration of the war.

●

Our intelligence officers had instructed us, if we were caught, to claim we were escapees and to back up this claim by inventing an escape story—even one in which we killed a guard, anything to make it sound plausible. If the Spaniards accepted our story, we could be home free. I myself had serious doubts about our ability to fool them, for I figured they could easily check us out with the Germans. So at all costs we had to avoid capture.

I, of course, had even greater cause than the others to fear capture by the Spanish Fascists. Not only had I fought in the ranks against Franco, but during my last seven months of service I was Political Commissar of the Lincoln Battalion, holding a rank equivalent to major. The commissar was an officer who carried the same rank and authority as the unit commander. His primary function was morale building and political education. Except for a very brief period, the Fascists had taken no International Brigaders alive, and even when they did take prisoners, officers were summarily shot. I was certain that I too would be executed if they discovered my identity. This was only four years after the victory of Franco over the Loyalists, and the bloodletting was still going on. Tens of thousands of vanquished Republican fighters were languishing in Franco prisons, and about half a million more had been forced into exile. Hundreds of executions were still being carried out. And guerrilla fighting was still raging in Asturias in the Basque region, in the very Pyrenees Mountains in which I was now hiding.

I thought about this while we were waiting for our guide to return. The irony of my situation did not escape me. The legendary La Passionaria (Dolores Ibarruri, an inspirational leader of the Republican cause and a Communist member of the Cortes, the Spanish parliament), in her farewell address to the International Brigades in Barcelona, had told us to come back to a free democratic Spain. We had shed our blood; we were legend, she said. Spain would be forever grateful to us. We were always welcome. Now I was back—but Spain was not free.

It was the suffering and tragedy of the Spanish Civil War that occupied my mind. I kept thinking of fallen comrades. The trauma of the defeat, which I had buried till now, resurfaced and enveloped me in sadness.

I did not share any of these thoughts and feelings with my companions during those long hours. And they may have wondered why I kept so silent most of that day. But I felt that I did not dare reveal any of this to the others. Johnson, of course, knew about my Spanish experience; all the men in my outfit in England knew. But I did not trust the Pole. He had been a career man in the Polish Air Force before the war. After the German and Soviet invasions of Poland he had enlisted in the Polish RAF, flying out of England. He had an intense hatred for the Soviets. At that time I was an ardent and uncritical believer in the Soviet system, and I felt duty bound to defend the Russians against his verbal assaults. Even from the vantage point of my later disillusionment with the Soviet Union, I would have taken issue with him then. The war against Hitler was far from over, and the Soviets were our allies, still fighting and sacrificing in the war against our common enemy. I felt his extreme hatred went beyond Polish nationalism. He defended the ruling aristocracy of Poland against the peasant and working-class movements; he held what I considered an extreme right-wing position on the social and political issues of the day. We had had many arguments from opposite ends of the political spectrum.

So while I admired his courage and would never take that away from him, I felt I could not trust him not to betray me if we were captured by the Spanish Fascists. I may have been wrong, but that's how I felt at the time. Not until we were safely out of Spain did I tell him that I had fought with the International Brigades. His face fell. He seemed taken aback. "I thought it was something like that," he said quietly. Those were the last words we spoke to each other during the remaining few days we spent together.

It was long after dark when our guide returned and told us we would be leaving the next morning to meet a car and chauffeur. We were awakened at dawn and began the arduous descent to our rendezvous, the snow making it especially treacherous and slippery. The going was easier after a couple of hours when we left the snow behind, except that now I could feel the jagged stones and pebbles on my left foot. But we made it down to a road, finally, and there we waited under cover until the car appeared.

When we were all safely inside, the driver attached a British flag to the fender. We were now in the custody of the British Embassy. At long last we were safe!

13

Spain Again

Safe at last? Franco's Fascist Spain could never be neutral for me—I was still in enemy territory.

The embassy car drove through San Sebastian and headed south toward Madrid. I had not been in this part of Spain before, but every terraced mountain, every olive grove, every hairpin turn brought back memories. We climbed a long mountain road. A vast breathtaking panorama opened before us. My eyes followed the wide valley to a distant village nestling against the far slope, and suddenly I remembered a strikingly similar scene in that earlier Spain of 1938.

It is dawn. Doran, Merriman, Wolff, Gates, and Lamb are standing on a mountaintop outside Villalba de los Arcos, gazing down the valley. It is an awesome sight. As far as the eye can see, on the road to our left and on the road to our right, endless columns of enemy tanks, artillery, and trucks are moving bumper to bumper into Gandesa, which nestles against the slope on the far side of the valley.

The day before, the enemy had broken through our flanks. We marched all night over rugged mountain trails to try to break out of encirclement. Now we know we didn't make it.

Puffs of white smoke rise over the city, and we hear the rumbling of artillery. A battle is raging. Doran orders an attack on Gandesa. It is daring, certainly suicidal, but we don't question the order. We feel duty bound to come to the aid of our Loyalist brothers still fighting in the city.

We begin to move to our left down the side of the mountain.

A sudden burst of machine-gun fire sends me diving for cover. Of all the stupid, idiotic . . . ! Why hadn't our scouts checked the ridge? The rapid tattoo of gunfire comes from above. We are sitting ducks.

Captain Wolff orders a retreat. The dirt kicks up around me as I get up to run. I make a mad dash to a piece of cover. My pack weighs a ton. It gets heavier every time I infiltrate from one spot to another. I haven't slept in thirty-six hours and am thoroughly exhausted. Strewn along the trails are my extra underwear and socks, toilet articles, books, mess kit, poncho. I still hold on to my rifle and bayonet, my ammo, and the one personal item I can't part with —my wife's letters.

Eight months of letters can slow a man down. They get heavier each time I run. Soon it's the letters or my life. I choose life. With great anguish, I pull out a handful and lay them tenderly behind a rock. I jump up to run again. Tsing, tsing, tsing. I don't wait to see how close they come. The weight of the pack still slows me. I drop another batch behind a boulder. Still no relief. Finally, I jettison the entire knapsack and make a frantic dash around a bend in the hill to safety.

For the next hour, Wolff, Gates, Lamb wait anxiously as the men appear one by one on the steep slope. Dave Doran, Political Commissar of the XVth International Brigade and the highest-ranking American officer in Spain, is one of the last. Halfway up he spots me and breaks into a broad grin. "My dearest beloved," Dave mocks when he reaches me. "Some hot love letters! I followed your trail and read every one of them." He laughs. I laugh along with him but want to dive into the nearest hole.

One-half of the battalion never make it back to the hill. They never make it back, period. They have been captured and massacred in the village plaza, we learn later from Spanish peasants.

We are back where we started that morning. But now the enemy knows we are there. We dig shallow foxholes behind the low terraced walls, determined to hold till nightfall and then try another run for the Ebro River.

It is a long and grueling day. The scattered olive trees do not provide enough shade to protect us from the hot sun. An enemy artillery battery opens fire. We crouch behind the parapets as we nervously watch the barrage creep up the hill toward us. The columns of Italian and German tanks, artillery, and troops continue to steamroller into Gandesa without letup.

Late in the afternoon we watch, horrified and helpless, as saber-swinging Fascist cavalry cut down our comrades who were sent to the adjacent hill to guard our right flank. After the bloody carnage the horsemen spread out in attack formation and ride at a deliberately slow pace down the valley toward our position. Our trigger fingers are itching to open up, but Doran orders us to hold our fire. They keep coming.

"Now!" Wolff pleads with Doran.

"Not yet," Doran says. They keep coming.

"Tira! Tira! Fire!" Wolff's booming shout overrides Doran.

Rifles and light machine guns open up. Horses and men tumble to the ground. They beat a retreat. It's a scene directly out of the movies. We feel great.

They regroup, and now twice as many let out bloodcurdling screams as they come charging at a full gallop. This time we don't wait. We open up with everything we've got. We cut them down again, and that ends that. It feels good to be shooting again after days of running.

We become aware that the puffs of smoke and the sound of artillery at Gandesa are gone. With a sinking feeling we realize that nothing will now stop the Fascists from reaching the Ebro River. For the first time in my own mind I face certain death. Captured International Brigaders are summarily shot by Franco's army. I'm determined to break out to freedom or go down fighting.

At night I am assigned by Gates to cover the rear of the column. I am completely isolated from everything up ahead. More than two hundred men are stretched out in single file in pitch blackness over the winding mountain trail. All I can see or feel is the man directly in front of me.

At times, I find myself running to keep up, deathly afraid of losing the column. We stop often, but I don't sit down for fear of falling asleep and letting the column move off without me. I never know why we stop. Are they waiting for the scouts to report? Are they lost? Has the column been broken?

I lose all sense of time. This is our third night without sleep. No change of socks—my feet are blistered. No food—all canned rations are gone. No water.

I awake with a start. I must have dozed off. I go up the line and confirm that we haven't moved in some time. I ask a rifleman to cover the rear, and I go forward to find out what has happened.

I find Johnny Gates, at that time the Lincoln Battalion's Political Commissar. None of the military commanders of the XV Brigade or the battalion are around. Johnny too is trying to learn what happened. "We heard some shots up ahead and everything stopped," he tells me. "We don't know where Merriman, Doran, and Wolff are."

"You're the top-ranking officer, Johnny. You've got to take charge," I urge. He has already reached that conclusion and needs no prodding from me. Gates sends out point scouts and, with me at his side, leads the forced march to the river.

Now I am wide awake. The adrenalin is working. Using the North Star to guide us, we walk rapidly toward the east, racing against the dawn. Gradually we leave the hills behind us and traverse the valley. We arrive at the road on which we earlier saw the Fascist trucks and tanks. We allow some vehicles to pass and wait for our scouts to report the road clear. Then we rush across.

We reach the Corbera-Gandesa road as dawn begins to

*break. On top of the hill to our left we see silhouetted figures
moving a machine gun into position. It's still dark in the valley,
and Johnny and I remain behind to rush the men forward. Too
late!*

"Oiga!" comes a shout from the top.

*"Oiga!" answers Lieutenant Copernico, a Spaniard who is
our battalion adjutant.*

"Quien es? Who are you?" they ask.

"Quien es?" he responds.

"Que bandera? What flag?"

*Now we know they're Fascists. The Fascists fight under many
flags and call their units* banderas. *They beckon Copernico
forward. He raises a white handkerchief and calmly strides up
the hill, continuing the conversation. The ploy works long
enough for our men to move forward. Most are out of range
when the machine gun opens up, but Gates and I are caught. We
outrun the traversing gunfire and head left up another hill.*

We reach the top only to hear that familiar "Oiga! Quien es?"

*Herman Lopez, a Puerto Rican comrade, shouts across the
ridge, "Fortificaciones." There's not a single pick or shovel
among us!*

*Lopez stalls them while Ralph Wardlaw, former CCNY in-
structor, and another rifleman flop down behind a mound to
cover our retreat. Bullets whistle past us as we duck behind the
crest of the hill and continue our flight.*

*Lt. Mel Offsink, company commander and former school-
teacher, sits down on the ground. "I can't go on."*

"Get up, Mel," I plead. "We've got to keep moving."

*"I can't move another step. I don't care what happens, my
feet gave out."*

*"You've got to. Please get up. Once you've stopped, you're
finished. You'll never get up." He can't budge.*

(We never heard from Mel again. Nor did Ralph Wardlaw or

the other rifleman make it. Herman Lopez, I later learned, was taken prisoner, but his life was spared because he pretended he was a Spaniard and not an International Brigader. Copernico, the Spaniard who surrendered to protect us Americans, walked into brigade headquarters three months later, laughingly demanding his back pay. He had escaped!)

I catch up with about a dozen men as we start to climb over the steep Sierra Caballs. A small plane spots us, and soon we are sniped at by artillery. I catch some shrapnel in my left hand, and while stopping to administer first aid to one of the more seriously wounded, I lose the column. I climb over the craggy crest and down the other side, this time completely alone. As I near the road, I hear the loud rumbling of tanks. I climb back up, make a wide detour over the mountain, and run into several other Lincolns.

We continue the descent into the river valley. While dropping down a terrace I sprain my ankle, and every step becomes agonizing. We find an abandoned farmhouse and help ourselves to ripe figs and sausages. Later some peasants offer more food and show us the best paths to the river.

In the late afternoon we reach our objective, the bridge at Mora del Ebro. To our dismay, all we find is twisted steel and broken concrete. The roar of the swollen torrent tells us emphatically that we are trapped.

Some of our guys can't swim, so we enter Mora del Ebro to look for a rowboat. The town is deserted, but in the mayor's office we find a handful of Spaniards waiting for the Fascists. They seem none too friendly. We learn from them that the bridge was blown only a couple of hours ago, after the last Republican columns marched across, and that all the boats were commandeered by the retreating Loyalists.

Joe Hecht, who speaks perfect Spanish, pulls his pistol. They stick to their story: there are no boats. Joe finally puts away his

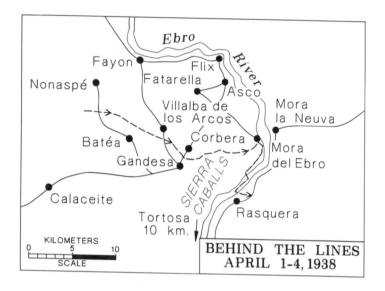

gun, and we continue our desperate trek down the bank of the roaring river.

It is beginning to get dark when we find an abandoned farmhouse. Our feet are sore and we are exhausted. We decide to bed down for the night. While the rest sleep, I stand guard. The hours drag. I hear someone start up the stairs. I move to the landing. He must have heard me because he heads down again. In the moonlight reflected through the open door, I recognize the silhouette of Johnny Gates. I yell, "Who's there?" My rifle is pointing at his back. Johnny is startled but recognizes my voice. It's a happy reunion. Johnny says he had a grenade ready, and we never do settle the good-natured argument as to who could have killed whom.

We merge our forces, his four men and our five. We tear the huge wooden door off its hinges and lash a log to each side. Captain Lenny Lamb comes by just as we're preparing to launch *the raft. He can't swim and refuses to join us. He will take his chances downstream.*

It's still dark when we launch the raft with its four non-swimmers. Two swimmers set out clinging to a log, but the current is too strong and they are forced to let go. Another man, Johnny, and I strip off all our clothes except for our berets, in which we place our military record books, and plunge into the swift icy waters. I'm a good swimmer but I am so thoroughly fatigued that I decide not to fight the current. As it carries me rapidly downstream, I hear a commotion behind me—then complete silence. I am horrified. I fear the worst for the men on the raft.

I am well downstream now, and it is light enough to see the shore. I see Johnny and make my way to his landing spot.

We walk stark naked and barefoot over a seemingly endless stretch of sharp stones and burrs that cut our feet. We are shivering from the cold, and our feet are bleeding when we reach the highway. But we are safe.

A truck comes down the road. I wonder what must be going through the mind of the driver, seeing two naked men standing on the highway. He hands us a couple of blankets and drives away without us.

A minute or two later a small black car screeches to a halt. Out come two men. We're damned happy to see them. One is Herbert Matthews, New York Times *correspondent; the other is Ernest Hemingway. We are the first Lincolns they've run into. No one has heard from the Lincolns in four days. The Lincolns are the lost battalion, they tell us.*

They ply us with questions. What happened? Where were we? How many got out? Where are Merriman and Doran? We are still dazed. We're just beginning to mourn our lost comrades. We're in no talking mood, but we tell them briefly what we know. Merriman and Doran ran into an ambush. We don't know whether they got away. There are hundreds of men still across

*the Ebro. Many are dead; some are drowned. How many cap-
tured? We have no idea.*

*Matthews is busy taking notes. Hemingway is busy cursing
the Fascists. He is angry. He is optimistic. The Republic is in a
fighting mood, stronger than ever, he tells us. The rear is
mobilized, and the Ebro is being fortified. The Fascists will not
cross the Ebro. We will get our revenge, he assures us. He talks
like one of us.*

*We rejoin our brigade and wait for the men to return. We soon
come to realize that most are not coming back. I feel alone.
Everyone close to me is gone. Max Kappie, my closest friend
when I was growing up. At fifteen, we read* All Quiet on the
Western Front *and swore we'd never go to war. This was his first
action, and now he is gone. Leo Kaufman, Irving Keith, Dave
Doran—gone.*

*But less than four months later Hemingway's prediction
comes true. We do get our revenge—for a time. The Lincoln
Battalion, as part of the greatest Republican offensive of the war,
recrosses the Ebro, retaking some of the ground where three-
quarters of our battalion was lost. This time we have the
rowboats we need.*

14

Over and Out

Such memories stirred strong feelings in me, and my excitement mounted as the embassy car approached Madrid. Madrid had been the heart and soul of the Spanish Civil War. It was here that La Passionaria rallied the embattled Madrileños with the cry "Better to die on your feet than live on your knees." It was here that the battle cry " *¡No Pasaran!* They Shall Not Pass!" was first shouted and became, for our generation, the "shot heard round the world." Here was where the first international volunteers joined Spanish youth holding back the Franco Fascists with pistols and pre–World War I rifles at University City. Here was where Hemingway held court at the Hotel Florida, to which flocked Americans on leave from the front, looking for good scotch, cigarettes, and a hot bath.

So Madrid was something special. And I was looking forward with great excitement to seeing it—for the first time. A year and a half in Spain, and I had never been to Madrid. I had seen Valencia and Barcelona but never Madrid. I had been in Spain ten months before receiving my first three-day pass from the front. By that time we were fighting in Catalonia, and we were cut off. So I had to settle for Barcelona—a beautiful city—but it wasn't Madrid.

My heart beat faster as we neared the city. It was already dark when we arrived, and to my great disappointment the driver headed straight for the British Embassy. I thought I had caught a glimpse of University City on the way in, but I couldn't be sure. Once again, I was fated not to see Madrid.

At the embassy we were ushered into an enormous hall lined with cots. A dozen men were lounging about, playing cards, reading, talking, getting haircuts and shaves. We were happy to see Pope and a few of the others we had met in that apartment back in Paris.

These escapees had arrived at the embassy four to seven days ahead of us and were getting ready for the trip to Gibraltar the next morning. So Johnson and I stayed only one night. Early the next day we all piled into two canvas-covered military trucks and left Madrid. We were escorted by a British Embassy official and a captain of the Spanish Internal Security Police. They rode in the cabs with the drivers of the trucks, while we, the escapees, were seated on wooden benches along the sides. It was not exactly the most comfortable ride, but we were on our way home.

After two hours on the road our two-truck convoy stopped for rest. As I jumped down, I came face to face with the Spanish Security Police captain. I had fought for a year and a half against the Fascist enemy but had never seen a live Fascist up close. The enemy was a nonperson to me. I knew his machine gun fire, his artillery, his antitank shells, and his aerial bombs—but not the man behind the gun or the cannon, or the aviator who strafed me from the air. I don't mean to say the fighting wasn't personal. It was damned personal. I had received a shoulder wound at Fuentes del Ebro. All around me my closest comrades were dying. I certainly felt that whoever was behind that trigger was out to destroy me personally. Only I never saw the "who" who was doing it.

I did see the enemy—but I saw him as a rotting corpse lying in the field, under the rubble of a bombarded town, or on the side of the road as battles seesawed back and forth. I could not relate to that stinking piece of decomposing flesh.

And during the Loyalist offensive across the Ebro River, the Lincolns had captured a company of Fascist troops. They were pitiful and very frightened young boys, wearing uniforms similar to our own and looking not very different from the *quintas* (conscripts) who were fighting on our side in the Lincoln Battalion. But the prisoners were taken to the rear, and I never got to talk to them.

So here I was facing the enemy in person for the first time—not a corpse or a frightened, disheveled youth marching abjectly to the rear but a living human being, an official of the Franco regime, undoubtedly a supporter of Hitler and Mussolini. He spoke English and acted as interpreter between the men and the Spanish shopkeepers. He was friendly and pleasant to all of us. I found it most unsettling. What should I do? Should I confront him? Should I snub him? While debating this with myself, I kept away from him during the first few stops.

After a while, however, I could no longer resist the temptation to talk to him. I asked if he had been in the civil war. Yes, he said, he was a sergeant in Franco's army. I asked him questions about the war, about armaments, about where he had fought. I may have betrayed a level of sophistication about ground combat not usually displayed by air force men, but he never caught on. And needless to say, I never mentioned that we had been on opposite sides. I remembered all too well that I was still inside Fascist Spain.

The rest of the trip was uneventful except for one pleasant stop at Jerez de la Frontera. There we were guests of the British consul, who wined and dined us in most luxurious fashion in a picture-postcard setting. Then we were taken to a large winery where the world-famous Dry Sack sherry was made. That same British consul was also the owner, and he took us on a tour of the factory, where we were told that the large oaken vats had been aged making whiskey in America for one hundred years before coming to Spain to make sherry; that the word "sherry" comes from the English vulgarization of "Jerez"; that Queen Victoria—or was it Prince Albert?—and other world dignitaries had visited and drunk the sherry from one of the ancient casks.

At which point our host dipped a long gold ladle into the barrel from which the queen had drunk and poured a glass of sherry for each of us commoners.

There were long lines at immigration and customs when we arrived at Gibraltar, but we were put through without a hitch and found ourselves on British territory. Now for the first time in forty-two days I could truly say and feel that I was safe at last. I had "walked out."

The Rock was jampacked with men and women from many countries, wearing uniforms of every description. In the small-world department, I ran into Si Podolin, a Spanish Civil War veteran and now a sea captain on a Liberty ship. There were bodies of men still floating in the flooded hold of his torpedoed ship, which was awaiting repairs in the Gibraltar harbor—a grim reminder of the big war I was coming back to.

After a few days Johnson and I were flown back to England on a Liberator, the B-24 that we B-17 men had derisively called the "Flying Coffin." We arrived at 8th Air Force Command in London on December 20. We were debriefed by a lieutenant from U.S. Military Intelligence and awaited identification by an officer from our squadron—the final security check meant to protect our side from penetration by a clever enemy spy. In the evening of December 22, a cheerful redheaded lieutenant came to vouch for us, and Johnson and I were free to walk out of the compound. Out of earshot of the others, the lieutenant laughingly said he didn't remember us at all; it had simply been his turn for a free trip to London. Whether he knew us or not was immaterial.

As Johnson and I stepped out into a fine London drizzle, an air raid siren went off. The searchlight beams diffusing through the haze, the rapid ack-ack of the antiaircraft guns, the loud wailing of the sirens sent chills up and down our spines.

"Boy, that would be the payoff," Johnson laughed nervously. "We go through all that goddamed flak, get shot down, escape the Gestapo, climb the Pyrenees, and get killed in a London air raid!"

We should have headed for a shelter. Instead, we quickened our pace toward the Rainbow Corner Red Cross near Marble Arch. The club was crowded as usual, but it wasn't the same crowd. The last time we'd been there, it was full of "fly boys," the glamorous airmen with their 8th Air Force shoulder patches, air medal ribbons with oak leaf clusters, silver wings pinned on the blue combat patch. Now it was ground forces and airborne infantry, cocky paratroopers with their jump boots and tough, rugged infantrymen. They wore no shoulder patches or distinctive insignia. The invasion I had promised the people in Zele and Hamme was coming, and the Allied command didn't want to make it easy for enemy spies to identify the units.

Many airmen looked down upon the infantryman, but even though I was now one of the fly boys, my heart was with the foot soldier, the guy who slogged it on the ground. In combat or at rest, he was never out of the war. He was wet and cold and hot and miserable all the time. He was dirty, lousy, and itchy and never too far from his own excrement. That was the war I had known in Spain. I was sure it was no different for the foot soldier in this one.

I had equal respect for the airman, however. Going from the safety and relative comfort of the air base into deadly combat within the space of a few hours brought its own brand of hell. The beginning of every mission was like the infantryman's "going over the top."

Now I looked at all these airmen, paratroopers, infantrymen, and tankists mingling at the club. I knew the frightful sacrifices that still lay ahead for them and for the men and women of the resistance. This was the fruition of everything my comrades and I had gone through from that first battle in Spain through the devastating retreats, the costly offensive across the Ebro, and the final tragic defeat of the Spanish people's fight for democracy.

Then, the overwhelming preponderance of force had been on the Franco, Hitler, Mussolini side. Now the shoe was on the other foot. I was more confident than ever that the final victory over Fascism was on the way.

I elbowed my way through the crowd to the Red Cross volunteer. Four days later, on December 26, 1943, Margie's gloomy Christmas turned to wild joy as she read my cable: "MERRY XMAS DARLING FEELING WONDERFUL YOU CANT GET RID OF ME LOVE—GEORGE WATT."

PART II. Going Back

15

Reunion in Hamme

May 1984—Belgium.

"Did you know I carried a gun and was prepared to shoot you after we left Dr. Proost's house?"

"No." I was startled.

"I thought you might be a German spy." Henri Malfait laughed, enjoying my astonished look.

This was a shocker to me. I thought that when he had radioed the answers on the questionnaire back to London, my identity had been confirmed, else why would he have taken me to his parents' home? Now Malfait told me he had not received a reply from London that evening and had to get me out of Dr. Proost's house in a hurry. Word finally did come the following day. But what if London had not been able to verify my identity? When I remember how files and communications sometimes get fouled up in the army, I shudder. I could have been shot!

This was not the only surprise awaiting us when Margie and I returned to Belgium for a four-day visit more than forty years after the event. Margie was as excited as I was at meeting the people she had come to know through my stories. What started as a long overdue expression of gratitude to people who had risked their lives for me and for so many others became an exciting voyage of discovery.

Before returning to Belgium, Margie and I had taken a seven-day barge trip on the canals of Holland, where we enjoyed the breathtaking beauty of the tulips at their peak. When we checked back into our hotel in Amsterdam, a letter was waiting. It began:

Dear George,

First of all I'd like to present myself because you have to know who is writing to you. My name is Monique Inghels. I'm Raymond's daughter. I was 3½ years old the 5th November 1943, the day you came down with your parachute in the fields of Durmen, the village where I lived with my parents.

Since that day I know you by name, because daddy told us often enough "the story of George Watt" and each time my brother and I were hanging on his lips.

I had wanted so much to see Raymond Inghels again, that irrepressible ship's cook who took me by tram and train to his in-laws, Dr. Jean Proost and his wife, Hedwige, in Brussels. Now I was too late. He had died fourteen years earlier of lung cancer. But Monique would take us to see the Proosts, her aunt and uncle.

I immediately called Monique in Hamme. The only time we could see her aunt and uncle was that very evening; they were leaving for Spain the next morning. There went Rembrandt, Vermeer, Hals, and all the Dutch painters we had come to see. We made a hurried visit to the Rijksmuseum and caught the 5:26 to Antwerp.

Monique, a tall, attractive, blonde woman, met us at the station with her husband, Theo, a robust man sporting a Van Dyke. A moment later I was surprised to see an older couple rushing toward us. By placing an imaginary cap on the man's head, I was able to recognize Eduard Lauwaert, the man with the cap, and his wife, Mathilde. We embraced and reminisced joyfully. Then Theo and Monique drove us to Brussels.

"George, you are very famous in Zele and Hamme. Everybody knows the story of George Watt," Monique said. "And everybody knows about Henri Malfait, the man who helped you, but I think he is dead. My father used to take us on picnics in the field where he was with you. Never in my wildest dreams did I imagine I would ever meet you. Now, it's a dream come true.

How sad that my father did not live to see you. After the war he sailed to New York many times and looked for you at your Long Island address but could not find you."

"What a shame. We moved to Manhattan soon after the war," I said.

When we arrived at her aunt and uncle's house, Hedwige greeted us. "This is where you stood forty years ago," she said as she closed the door behind us. I remembered that first frightened look and thought of the heroism of a young doctor's wife who risked everything to protect an American airman who was a complete stranger to her.

Dr. Proost came down the stairs, a handsome, gray-haired man looking considerably younger than his seventy years. After we embraced, he showed us the room on the ground floor where Raymond and I had stayed in hiding all that day.

"I heard Malfait is dead," I said. "I feel very sad that I missed him."

"Oh, no, no. Malfait is alive," Dr. Proost said. I was overjoyed.

As we began to relive that day forty years before, Dr. Proost told us a few things I had not known: that I was Malfait's first "client"; that Proost's wife was in the beginning of her pregnancy when I arrived with Raymond; that a three-volume book on the Belgian resistance, published in French a few years earlier, recounted the incidents of my rescue. The doctor further revealed that his sister Marguerite had worked with Malfait as typist for the underground newspaper *La Libre Belgique*. It was through her that he knew Malfait—a stronger connection than he had indicated to me in 1943.

Dr. Proost recalled how we plotted my route to the French border on a map printed on the silk handkerchief that came with my escape kit. And he remembered going out in a cold downpour to look for Malfait.

When Margie, toward the end of our visit, said we were Jewish, it was like telling the Proosts they had just been anointed in heaven. "All these years I was happy to have helped save an American flyer," Dr. Proost said, his face lighting up with a beautiful smile. "Now that I know I helped save a *Jewish* American flyer, I feel even happier.

"During the war I knew a dentist who was Jewish. One day he was returning from a visit to a friend. He walked down the street carrying his briefcase against his chest to hide the yellow star he was forced to wear. As he approached his house, a neighbor came up to him and said, 'Don't go home. The Gestapo came and took your wife and child away.'

"For the rest of the German occupation he stayed with small groups of Jews who were hiding in private homes scattered through Brussels. They were able to live because people helped them with ration stamps and food. My sister Marguerite used to collect food stamps for Malfait, who distributed them to resistance people, to Jews, and to others in hiding.

"The Germans came to our hospital director, Dr. Titeca, and demanded to search the institution for Jews. He refused to allow them in: 'They are patients. They stay in my institution. You don't touch them.' And the Germans never took them," Dr. Proost concluded with pride.

On Sunday morning we went to the Lauwaerts' house, the same house in which I had stayed when Mathilde brought me from the cold, dark outhouse where I was forced to hide until they had put their child to bed. A large American and large Belgian flag draped the windows. All the Lauwaerts' children and grandchildren and Yvonne Inghels, Raymond's widow, were there, as well as Monique and a number of villagers.

The secretary of the village of Hamme made a short speech, and I spoke briefly. I said that I had come back to thank each one in person for the heroic acts they had performed on my behalf and on behalf of liberty. I mentioned Eduard and Mathilde Lauwaert, Raymond Inghels, and Leon Ducolumbeir (the little old man) and his wife, both deceased. I was presented with a plaque bearing the Hamme coat of arms, and Margie with a bouquet of roses. The Lauwaerts gave me a book in Flemish by Etienne Quintyn called *Tussen Pletwals en Bookhamers* (*Between the Hammer and the Anvil*, Zele, 1940-45), and showed me the section dealing with my rescue. It was titled, "Zijn verjaardag" (His birthday). They had remembered!

"Do you recognize this?" Mathilde showed me a dogtag, and I felt the oddest sensation. There was my name and serial number and Margie's name and address. It had remained hidden in their house all through the occupation. Suddenly I saw the letter "H" positioned in the lower right-hand corner. "H" stood for Hebrew. I had completely forgotten it was there! How stupid of me. I should have warned Eduard to discard it when I took the other one that morning at Ducolumbeir's house. The penalty for aiding a downed Allied flyer might be death, but for helping a Jew it was certainly death.

Ironically, I had carried that dogtag in my shoe all across Nazi-occupied Europe to protect me, if caught—without it, I could have been labeled a spy. But with it, I now realized, I might just as well have worn the yellow star of David on my chest. Some choice!

I was startled further when Monique handed me a silk handkerchief with a finely embroidered floral pattern. "This is a piece of your parachute, George." I hadn't realized that villagers had cut off pieces of the parachute before the gendarme took it.

"You keep it."

"No, I have another one," she said. "My mother's aunt made two of them."

After a four-hour lunch in a pleasant restaurant, we all—four carloads of us—drove to the field where I had come down. On the way we stopped to see the farmer who owned the land, the one I had dubbed "the stump." Wies (Alois) Van den Bossche was quite old now, and his face was fuller, but as he came hobbling toward me on two canes, I recognized him at once. He was unmistakably the stump.

When he learned who I was, he gave me the same broad smile, but this time he talked a blue streak. He seemed to remember everything that had happened and a bit more. "You said, 'I am an American.' You said it in French. *Je suis americain. Je suis american,'* " Weis said.

Later, we tried to get to the spot where I had landed. But what with the women wearing high heels, and the children, and the fields being muddy and rutty, and Eduard having an asthma attack, we had to scrub that mission.

Next morning I was invited to speak at the elementary school. The children rewarded us with a delightful song in English, which they had rehearsed that morning, and a ten-year-old girl sang "Doodle-ee-doo," rolling her eyes like a flapper of the Roaring Twenties.

In the evening Monique drove us to Brussels to see Malfait. I had some trepidation about meeting the man who, I had learned, had been brutally tortured by the Gestapo because of his help to me and other airmen, but my uneasiness dissipated when I saw the smiling Henri waiting for us in front of his house. I could feel his warmth as we threw our arms around each other. He was no longer the skinny youth full of nervous energy; his face was now rounder, and his hair was graying. He had a gentle, serene look, masking a severe coronary condition and other ailments resulting from his concentration camp experience. His wife, Madeleine, was a frail and gentle woman who spoke no English but listened intently as we talked.

Margie, Monique, and I sat entranced as Malfait launched into his story immediately after he dropped that bombshell about the gun. Two months after my departure from Brussels he had been arrested by the Gestapo.

The indescribable horrors and bestiality of the Nazis came

alive for us as we listened to Henri's account of torture by repeated "drownings" and beatings. "They drowned me three times. They put my head in the tub and kept it there till I passed out. Before each drowning they beat my shoulders with a club, a special club called *nerf-de-boeuf*, bull's penis. The pain was so bad I couldn't breathe. Then, when I was terribly weakened and scarcely conscious, they asked me questions: what I did, if I recognized this one or that one, and so on and so on. When I didn't answer or gave a false answer, they did it again. They were going to do it a fourth time, but they accidentally hit my head and cracked it open. There was so much blood, they were afraid to put my head in the tub again, so they began beating me on my heart. I was standing up against the wall, and they beat me till I fell. Then they became concerned that they might kill me, so they bandaged my head. I don't know how long it lasted. I can't tell."

After this "interrogation" at Gestapo headquarters, Henri and Jules Dricot, his chief, were transported to the Fort Breendonk concentration camp, near Antwerp, where they were kept standing in one of the passageways all night with their arms raised. "When I tried to lower my arms, I received a blow in my back. The next morning they shaved my head, gave me a prison uniform, and put me in solitary confinement, where I stayed for six weeks. I was let out of my cell only once a day, to empty slop pails. They threw a black cloth hood over my head so I couldn't see, and as I carried two slop pails down the narrow corridor, the guard would beat me across my shins with a club." He raised his right trouser leg, revealing the ugly blue scar that still covered his shin, forty years later.

"I will go to Breendonk," I said impulsively.

"Yes?" Malfait sounded surprised.

"Why are you surprised?"

"They don't usually go there." But I could see that Henri was pleased.

"How did you feel when you were arrested? Were you expecting it?

"It was terrible. We knew from the beginning that someday it would come. Every time we had an airman with us, and every time we made a visit to a German facility, you can believe it, we were always expecting to be arrested. When we distributed *La Libre Belgique,* we could be arrested also. Yes, it was terrible because it was finished for us. Couldn't do any more.

"I was arrested at Madame De Bruyn's house. The Gestapo didn't come to my parents' till later in the evening. They surprised them by letting themselves in with my key. My mother was sitting at the dining room table mending a robe. The Germans said, 'Don't move!' while they went to search the house. My mother suddenly remembered a tin box resting on the cupboard in full view. She quickly threw the robe over the box. 'Don't move!' the German shouted.

" 'Excuse me,' my mother said very calmly and took back the robe with the box hidden inside. They never did find the box. And that was marvelous because in that box were false identities, food stamps, and a report on German installations ready for wireless transmission to London. They never connected my parents to my activities, and the Gestapo never bothered them after that."

In April 1944 Malfait was sentenced to death but by some fluke escaped execution and was transferred to the concentration camp at Buchenwald. There he was surprised to see German political prisoners who had opposed Hitler. "That is why I myself do not criticize the German. I criticize the Nazi. It is very different. In the earliest days of Hitler it was mainly German Communists and Socialists who were arrested. And there were Catholics too.

"Of course we know the Communists had done a lot of things. I recognize that. A lot of them were prisoners, and they let the world know that they were victims. But they don't speak of all the advantages they had in concentration camp."

"Advantages? What advantages?"

"You know, toward the end of the war, the Germans needed all their men at the front, so they put German prisoners in charge of running the camps. And who were these German prisoners? Mostly Communists, though a few common criminals were also appointed because they were German. They were the block leaders and were on the *arbeit statistic,* which controlled all work assignments.

"I was sent as a *kommando* to Halberstadt, 100 kilometers from Buchenwald—you heard about *nacht und nebel,* night and fog? It means that you go to this *kommando* and nobody knows about you afterward. You never come back alive. There were Belgians, Poles, and Jews, of course in these *kommandos,* But I did not see one Communist there. Because we were chosen by *arbeit statistic,* And *arbeit statistic* was controlled by the Communists."

"What you're telling me, concerns me very much, Henri," I said, "because in those days, I was a Communist."

"Yes?" Henri's eyes opened in surprise.

"Yes. I was a Communist then. I left the movement much later, after I became convinced that Stalin was a tyrant and after the invasion of Hungary. But during the war and after the war, I was a Communist. I was idealistic, and I believed we were building a new society."

"Of course," Henri interjected.

"And before I got into this war, I had fought in the Spanish Civil War."

"So?!" Henri's eyes popped wide open.

"Yes, I was in the International Brigades. I guess you've heard about them."

"Oh yes!" Henri turned to Madeleine and translated this last bit of dialogue. They nodded their heads, smiling at me approvingly.

"I fought in Spain for a year and a half. So when you tell me these things—from my own experience, I've known about the heroism and sacrifices of Communists."

"Of course, that's true!" Henri added emphatically.

"And I've known of Communist misdeeds, but these stories about the camps I hadn't heard, and they disturb me."

"That's my feeling. And I understand they did it because they had the possibility to do it. They were chosen by the Germans because they were the first prisoners and were there the longest. Perhaps if another part of the German population—for example, if all the Catholics had been in concentration camps before the others—perhaps they would have done the same."

But Malfait also vented his feelings against the Communists for hogging the credit. "They talk like nobody else was in the resistance. I have here a book on Buchenwald. It is a very big book. Many of the details in it are right. But they left out some important things. Why? Because it's written by Communists. For example, there was a certain priest in Buchenwald called 'Father Lulu.' After his release he published a book about the camp. It was written in verse. Because he was not permitted to write while in camp, he composed verses in his head and memorized them by repeating them over and over. This history of Buchenwald, written by the Communists, has a bibliography of all the titles of books written on the camp—but it doesn't mention the priest's book. That's a pity. For me it's a pity."

"I can understand your feelings," I said. "I remember when I met you and your family in 1943, you made a very profound impression on me. You broadened my horizons, making me think about the resistance in more complete terms."

"That is my opinion," Malfait added. "What I told you doesn't diminish the resistance of the Communists, you see, but they were not the *only* ones."

The *kommando* life, building an underground factory in Halberstadt, was extremely brutal, and Malfait developed a severe chronic stomach ailment. "But I survived. I began to reevaluate my entire life, and I was able to survive because two strong beliefs sustained me. One was my belief in God. And the other was my belief in love. Do you know the definition of love? It may be different things for different people, but for me love is being able to help someone, even if you don't know that person. And then you have such satisfaction to have done something to make others free. I believe that is the most important thing, to give freedom to others and to be free myself, of course."

During our remaining two days in Hamme we found the ditch where I had spent most of that first afternoon, we met the "man with the footprints," whose tracks on the plowed field had led the Germans away from my hiding spot, and we visited the site of the tram station, which is now a bus stop and a parking lot. But we searched in vain for the "beautiful redhead" to whom I had given my leather flight jacket. Then there was "the man with the cow": legend had it that the Germans missed me because a farmer had hidden me behind the rump of a cow he was taking to Durmen that day. I never did see a cow, but tracking down the story led to the solution of one mystery. The man with the cow was Omer Van Hecke; it was he and his sister Celine who had come to me in the ditch and invited me to their house. For forty years I had wondered whether they were in the underground.

"When you invited me to your home, what did you have in mind?" I asked Omer and Celine.

"To feed you. You looked so hungry."

"Nothing else? You weren't going to hide me?"

"Oh, no. Our house is right in the field. The Germans would have come to look for you there. It was much too dangerous."

I had made the right decision, after all, in sticking with Raymond.

When we first arrived, I had asked Monique, "Do you know the policeman who let me get away? I'd like to see this man."

"He was a collaborator!" Monique burst out.

"But he let me get away. And I want to thank him."

"You can't, because he's dead. His name was Leon Famaey. He let you go because he was afraid the people would kill him. His own sister Susanne said, 'Let him run. The occupation will not last forever. If you turn him in, you will not be able to live in this village. You will not be able to live with your own family.'"

In all the years that I had told the story to anyone who cared to listen, I had related how I finally mustered my fighting spirit and made an impassioned plea to the Belgian *gendarme* not to turn me in. I had taken the credit for persuading him. Now I learned it wasn't my eloquence that moved him. He had in truth been wrestling with two fears: fear of his Nazi boss, and greater fear of the retribution of the villagers. This brought me down a peg.

After the war Famaey was brought before the tribunal as a collaborator, charged with a number of offenses against the people. He had one defense: on 5 November 1943, at great risk to himself, he had saved an American flyer by not turning him over to the Germans. And so he escaped the maximum penalty. "You, George, saved his life," Monique said. "If not for you he would have rotted in jail and been run out of the village."

A poignant postscript to the Famaey story has to do with Albert Van Eetvelder—Jan—who had come with Raymond to visit me in the ditch. The next day Leon Famaey had come to Jan and said, "You better watch out. I know you were with the American. I'm going to watch you."

"I got so scared that the next day I signed up to work in Germany and didn't return till after the war, a year and a half later." Jan choked with emotion just remembering how frightened he'd been.

After exchanging gifts with the Lauwaerts, the Inghels, and their neighbors in Hamme and after prolonged goodbyes Margie and I left to carry out the promise I had made to Malfait. I had read about the concentration camps, but that didn't prepare me for what I was to experience at Fort Breendonk. To get to

Malfait's cell, we had to walk over wet cobblestones through a dark, dank, cold tunnel. I looked through the peephole into No. 7, where Malfait had been kept in solitary. It was no more than five feet wide and six feet long, one of sixteen cells in a room 15 by 40 feet. In a barracks room the same size, forty-eight people had slept on three-tiered straw mattresses. Then we saw the torture chamber. We couldn't get out of there fast enough!

16

Homage to the Comet Line

In 1985 Margie and I returned to Belgium. This time we spent four weeks instead of four days and were able to tie up important loose ends.

Finding the Thibauts, the couple with the baby, at whose house I had stayed for eight days, was one piece of unfinished business. In 1984 I had seen their pictures in Malfait's copy of Colonel Remy's book *Réseau Comète*—Raoul and Marie holding baby Inès—but my joy had immediately turned to grief when Malfait told me that the symbol next to Raoul's name meant he had died in a concentration camp. Then, several months later, he wrote me that it was Marie Thibaut who had died in concentration camp Ravensbrück in March 45. "Raoul died two years ago," he wrote, "but little Inès was caught with her mother by the Gestapo on 23 January 1944."

But when we saw Henri Malfait again in 1985, he greeted me excitedly: "I have wonderful news for you. Raoul Thibaut is alive! And he lives right here in Brussels." Ten minutes later Margie and I were in our rented car racing to the other end of Brussels to meet him.

I did not recognize him. The Raoul I remembered, the one in the photograph, had a sharp angular face and a full head of red hair. Now his face was round and his hair very thin. His voice had not changed, but his English was not as fluent as it had been forty-two years earlier. Neither was my French. We had a hard time conversing, but we managed.

I learned the tragic story of Marie's arrest. On January 22,

1944, a Saturday, Thibaut's servant spotted Gestapo agents on the street below and signaled Raoul. Robert Hoke, an American airman, was hiding in the same apartment at 134 Avenue du Diamant where I had stayed only two months earlier. Raoul and Hoke scooted down a back stairway into the garden, jumped over two walls, and got away. The Gestapo waited all afternoon and night for Raoul to return. Sunday at noon, when they realized he wasn't coming back, they took Marie with her baby to Gestapo headquarters. Thibaut's voice dropped with a soft sob as he finished telling this story.

I didn't ask any questions.

Margie and I talked about our children and grandchildren, and Raoul took out some family pictures. "There's my wife" (after the war he had married Jenny Roehrig). "She was also in the resistance and in Ravensbrück concentration camp with my first wife, Marie. She has been ill for the last years," Raoul said. "She's in the hospital. It's a result of the concentration camp. She suffered very much."

He continued with the photographs. "There's my mother. This is my sister. This is my daughter."

"Your daughter? Which daughter?" My pulse quickened.

"Inès. I have only one daughter."

"Inès? The baby I played with?"

"Of course."

"But I thought she was dead. I heard the Gestapo took her away with Marie and no one knew what became of her."

"She was taken with my wife to Gestapo prison. But when they were getting ready to deport Marie to concentration camp, the officer asked her if she had someone to leave the baby with. Since I was in hiding, they sent Inès to Marie's aunt, who raised her till after the war."

"This is like a fairytale," I said. "My head is spinning. First I had heard that you were dead. Then I heard it was Marie who was dead and that Inès had disappeared in the camps. Now, in the space of two hours, I learn not only that you are alive but that Inès is alive also. You have no idea how happy I am."

When I told Raoul that I was writing a book on my experience with the Belgian underground, he readily agreed to be interviewed on tape, and we set a date for the Monday after Margie and I would return from a visit to Madame Ugeux in southern France.

Though I had never heard of Madame Ugeux until a few months before, her name proved to be central to my story. When I left Belgium in 1984, the biggest unresolved question was the nature of the organization that had rescued me in 1943. Was it based on the British intelligence network left over from World War I, as we had been told in briefings? Was there one organization in Belgium and another in France, as I had assumed at the time? Who were these people who had risked their lives so that I and others could be free?

Then, in reading everything I could find on the Belgian and French resistance, I ran across a book called *Comète: Une histoire d'une ligne d'evasion* (*Comet: A History of an Evasion Line*), by Cecile Joan. As soon as I found references to "safe houses" in Brussels, crossing the Franco-Belgian border, layovers in Paris, travel to southern France, and climbing the Pyrenees into Spain, I knew I had struck paydirt. And imagine my excitement when near the end of the book the name "S/Sgt George Watt" jumped out of the page. I was the sixtieth American in a list of RAF and American airmen rescued by the Comet Line.

The names of three women kept appearing in the history of the Line: Andrée de Jongh (Dédée), Elvire de Greef (Tante Go—named for her dog, Go Go), and Micheline Lily Ugeux (Michou). Dédée was the founder of the Comet Line. Tante Go, at St. Jean-de-Luz, was its chief in the foothills of the western Pyrenees. Michou was personally involved in the rescue of 150 airmen. Intrigued by the reports of their organizational skills, resourcefulness, and courage, I wanted very much to meet these women. Unfortunately, Dédée was too ill to see us. I was not able to reach Tante Go. And Michou, by the time we got to Belgium in 1985, had retired with her husband, Pierre, to their villa in southern France near Avignon. We made plans to meet her there.

Michou is physically small but carries herself with such straight-backed dignity that one gets the impression of a much taller person. Her hair is graying; her face remains youthful. She talks about the most daring and traumatic experiences in a soft and gentle voice. There is no mistaking her quiet strength.

Sitting on her patio looking down on the beautiful church steeple and lush valley of St. Siffret, Michou showed us a huge album. "Do you know these men?" she asked, pointing to two passport-size pictures.

"Of course! This is Johnson and that is Maiorca!" I was so astonished that I neglected to ask how she knew they were members of my crew.

"I made these identity photographs. I was involved with both of them."

In Johnson's Evasion and Escaping report, which I had procured from the National Archives in Washington, he had mentioned being escorted by "Lily" and again meeting "Lily" at the train station in Brussels before taking off for the French border. Now I made the connection: "Lily" was Michou.

In August 1942 Michou's father, mother, and sister Nadine were arrested by the Gestapo. It was often the practice of the Gestapo to round up whole families. But Michou escaped arrest because, as a student nurse living at St. Jean Berchman's College in Brussels, she was not on her family's ration stamp list.

"I went to the Germans to ask permission to visit and write to my parents and sister. The German said, 'These are not your parents. We arrested the entire family, so you can't be in the family.' I had to go to the town hall to get proof that I was one of the daughters before they let me see them."

Michou's mother was released after thirteen months, but her sister and father were deported to a concentration camp in Germany. "My sister came back from Montosa after the war in very bad health. My father was in Silesia when the Russians approached. There was no time to evacuate the prisoners. So the Germans set fire to the camp and to the trains into which they had loaded the people."

"With the people in them?" I couldn't conceal the horror in my voice.

"Ah yes. The people who stayed in the camp were burned. They burned the trains with the people inside. By the time the Russians came, my father was finished. Yes . . . "

Michou's voice trailed off into a soft sigh. There was a long pause before we continued.

Nadine had been working with the Comet Line since mid-1941, so after the family's arrest, Michou took her sister's place. In her time off from nursing duties she took flyers to be photographed for false identification papers and did escort work.

"In June 1943 two German spies posing as American flyers penetrated our organization. As a result there were forty arrests. It was too dangerous for me to remain in my nursing job. I left the hospital, went underground, and worked full time for the airmen from then on."

Within a year Michou had become a legend among the flyers. She did everything from procuring housing to escort work, ration stamp collecting, and recruiting members and rebuilding the Line after arrests. Through it all she managed to keep out of the clutches of the Gestapo.

The list of arrests in the Comet Line was staggering.

"In June 1943, you had forty-two arrests," I said. "That must have been a terrible blow."

"Yes, but in August 1942 it was 138."

"One hundred thirty-eight!? In Brussels and Paris?"

"Oh no, no, no! In Brussels alone. From June 1941 to September 1944, when Belgium was liberated, there were 1,300 arrests in the Comet Line."

Talk about casualties! In the U.S. National Archives I had obtained Michou's report to American Intelligence made in September 1944. Here is an excerpt:

June 1943: On the 7th of June 1943 Paris blows up. . . . Paul was arrested and shot. Baby (Robert Hayle) was arrested and shot. . . . Raymonde Gouache was arrested, condemned to death and deported to Germany. Madeleine (wife of Baby Hayle) was arrested, condemned to death and deported to Germany. On the 8th of June, Brussels blows up. . . . Radlet is arrested and condemned to death."

The list of arrests and executions goes on and on. Then, in January 1944: "Jacques De Bruyn is arrested. Mme Francoise is arrested. Jeanne, Beatrice, Marie-Louise, Roland are arrested. . . . Brussels blows up. M. Deltour, Mme de Bruyn, Mme Thibaut, Henri Malfait, Eli Mirroir are arrested."

The names were no longer unfamiliar. Jacques De Bruyn had taken me from Malfait's house to his mother, Madame De Bruyn. Marie-Louise was the short guide dressed in black who escorted us from the Gare du Nord to that crowded apartment in Paris and later played the lover's tryst scene with H.C. Johnson on the banks of the Seine. Madame Thibaut, whose dynamism and intense conviction I could never forget, was the wife of Raoul and the mother of Inès, the baby I had played with. And, of course, Henri Malfait . . . I had known these people, and their arrests had come only two months after they helped me.

"What do you do, Michou, how do you feel after Brussels or Paris 'blows up'?" I asked.

"At first we are very *malheureuse*. It is very hard, especially when it is our friends. But after that we must continue to work more. The war goes on. And the flyers don't stop falling. We must go on. It is our mission. We begin to rebuild the Line."

"How?"

"In Brussels we recruited people we knew. But in Paris in March 1944 the Gestapo got everyone, and I was alone. I got some names from the British and started again."

"What kind of people were they?"

"Every kind. When Nemo [Baron Jean Greindl, head of the Line after Dédée's arrest] was there, there was lots of nobility and *haute bourgeoisie*. But after that the people, especially those who provided shelter, were from the very poor. You know, the very poor were very proud and in the beginning did not receive any money. But afterward, when the Line was well organized, they were paid for food.

"People never said, 'I am Socialist or Catholic or Communist.' And in Belgium the Communists were very strong in the resistance. And there were the French-speaking, the Dutch-speaking, no problem."

"How did you manage to stay out of the clutches of the Gestapo?"

"I knew a lot of people and moved around a lot. I never stayed in one place, and so I was always alone. Also I was lucky."

Of course, luck is important; I've always said my own escapes and survival were due 98 percent to luck. But Michou added to her luck with cleverness, cool-headedness, self-discipline, and total dedication. Plus the fact that she looked and acted like a fifteen-year-old.

"In March 1944 I was in Bayonne in the south of France when contact with Brussels was broken off after the last arrests. M. Cresswaith, the British MI-9 chief in Madrid, asked me if it was possible to reestablish contact. I said, 'No problem.' And I went to Paris. But the railroad was bombed by the Americans, and I had to change for a bus, arriving in Paris very late. When I phoned to say I am late, a strange woman's voice answered. It was not my friend Martine, so I knew she was arrested. Because the train was bombed, I was lucky."

Granted, that was luck. In other instances too, Michou had called ahead and learned of arrests. But there were just as many times when it was her uncanny sense for spotting spies or her quick thinking that got her out of a jam. "Fifty times or more," says her U.S. Intelligence file,

Madame Ugeux outwitted the German agents by suddenly enacting a tender, tearful love scene in a streetcar or on a station platform with some airman she had only known for an hour or two. Encountering such a scene, the embarrassed German agent would pass on and ask no questions. . . . At last the Gestapo did learn who the famous 'Michou' really was . . . but she brilliantly eluded their trap. She had been called to a rendezvous at the home of a Comet member, but Madame Ugeux first placed a telephone call and discovered, as she expected, that it was the Gestapo waiting for her. On another occasion she suddenly became suspicious of an aviator she had gone to pick up. To test him before revealing herself, she used the latest slang she had learned from other aviators. . . . his bewilderment in the face of the slang words convinced Madame Ugeux that she was dealing with a German agent.

In March 1944 Michou was actually arrested and placed in the Fresne prison in Paris, but "I was there only two days. The commandant thought I was too young, so he let me go before the Gestapo came to take me." Monique Thomé, the Comet member who had guided Johnson and me over the Belgian border into France in 1943, vividly described to me later how cleverly babyish Michou had acted in the Fresne prison.

When Michou returned from Bayonne to Paris and learned that Martine had been arrested, she suspected that there was a traitor inside the Line and was determined to find out who. "So I went to the prison in Fresne. In prison Martine said the traitor was Pierre, the same boy who was responsible for the arrests in June. Jean Masson, Pierre Boulain is the same boy, *oui*, the traitor."

"His real name was Jacques Desoubrie," I said, showing off, proud that I had done my homework. Jacques Desoubrie, alias Jean Masson, alias Pierre Boulain, kept coming back like a bad penny. As Masson, he infiltrated the Brussels organization in June 1943. After causing the arrests of Frédéric de Jongh, Dédée's father, and thirty Comet members in Brussels, he disappeared from sight until January 1944, when he appeared in Paris under the name of Boulain, brazenly claiming not only that he had worked for de Jongh but that he had been charged with eliminating Jean Masson!

"One day after the war," Michou went on, "Lt. Harold Cherniss, the American Intelligence officer, telephoned me and said, 'Michou, you must come quickly.' I went to Harold's office and he showed me twelve little pictures of identity cards and asked, 'Do you know that boy?' I said, 'Yes. This is Jean Masson and it is Pierre Boulain.' He said, 'Michou, it is very important. Please look carefully.' I said, 'No problem. Pierre Boulain, Jean Masson, the same boy.' He laughed. I said 'What happened, Harold?' 'That boy is working for the Americans in Nuremburg!'"

But not for long. Desoubrie/Masson/Boulain was tried and executed at Lille in 1945.

Michou was proud of the independence of the Comet Line. Andrée de Jongh, the young Belgian nurse who founded the organization in 1941, set the tone: "Dédée, Tante Go, and I, we were all of the same opinion. We are Belgian and we would like one day Belgium to be free. Dédée never wanted to be controlled by the English." They accepted money from the English, but it was on a per capita basis, for the number of airmen delivered into Spain, and then only for food and travel expenses.

When the Gestapo was closing in and Michou could no longer operate in Brussels, she still refused to leave the Comet Line. She transferred her operation to Paris and made five trips with aviators across the Pyrenees into Spain. Dédée had made at least eighteen round trips across those mountains—and I had sworn "never again" after my second crossing! So I felt a little sheepish when I said to Michou, "You know, I climbed the Pyrenees twice."

Michou looked puzzled.

"In 1937 I climbed the Pyrenees to get into Spain to join the International Brigades."

Michou's face lit up. She called to Pierre to tell him animatedly in French that I had fought in the Spanish Civil War. Pierre also became excited. He smiled warmly at me and told us of a close friend who had served with the International Brigades: "He was a doctor—the surgeon who operated on Michou after the war. You know she had a terrible condition with her stomach, the years of living so badly, moving around, not eating properly. He was a very good doctor and a very fine person."

Pierre Ugeux, who retired as director of the Belgian Power Authority, was working with British Intelligence in London when Michou arrived there in 1944. (She was *brûlé,* hot, and could no longer be useful on the Continent) They fell in love and were soon married. He was involved in several dangerous parachute drops into Nazi-occupied Europe, but he says little about his wartime experience. In fact, he and Michou talked so little about the war at home that not until Michou was written up in the papers as a leader of the Comet Line did their daughter hear the story in school. "Daddy," she asked that night, "why didn't you and mother tell us about what you did in the war?"

"We want to forget the war," Pierre said to his daughter—and to Margie and me.

Michou, Dédée, and Tante Go each received the U.S. Medal of Freedom, with Gold Palm, the highest award presented to civilians in World War II.

The morning after we returned from Avignon, I called Thibaut to confirm our date. A tearful voice answered the phone. "George, George. I'm very sorry. I can't see you. My wife died."

He began to sob. "She died while you and Margie were at my house. I am leaving shortly to go to my sister."

So I never did get a chance to tape the Thibaut story. But the Modern Military Branch of the National Archives provided me with the family's dossiers. As members of the Comet Line, the Thibauts' job was *hébèrgement,* housing and feeding, and Raoul sometimes escorted flyers to the French border. They also belonged to Service Zero, an intelligence branch of the resistance. Between September 1, 1943, and January 23, 1944, when the Gestapo raided their home, they had housed ten flyers. During those four months there was hardly a moment when a flyer wasn't hiding in the Thibaut apartment. Raoul was cited by the U.S. War Department for his level-headedness not only in slipping that last aviator out of the house but in retrieving important incriminating documents so that the Nazis did not get hold of them. One possible incriminating item is not referred to as such in his report: "I have in my possession the watch of George Watt engraved in his honor; it carries the same importance as an identity inscription." I had completely forgotten giving him my watch.

What Raoul did after his wife's arrest, I do not know. But he is listed in December 1945 at the time of the report as "Capt. Raoul Thibaut."

About Marie Thibaut, U.S. Military Intelligence has this to say:

On January 22, 1944 while her husband, Raoul Thibaut succeeded in fleeing with the American aviator Robert Hoke . . . thanks to her sang-froid and her remarkable energy, [she] succeeded in saving all the documents, archives and all material of the Service [Zero], necessary for the repatriation of allied airmen. . . . During her captivity at Saint Gilles and in Germany, Madame Thibaut had an extremely courageous attitude . . . the reports of all her companions returning from the camps agree with this."

So does the Citation for the Medal of Freedom awarded by the U.S. War Department to "Marie-Rose Thibaut, Belgian Civilian": "The courage, bravery, and exceptional devotion to the common cause of freedom displayed by this person in undertaking such hazardous duties, knowing the price to be paid if apprehended, were a definite contributing factor to the termination of hostilities in this theatre, meriting the highest degree of praise."

One last mystery that I was able to clear up concerns the lampoon edition of *Le Soir* and how the underground had pulled off so bold a feat. Through a journalist acquaintance working at *Le Soir* I was allowed to see the documents on that incident from the newspaper's morgue. The firsthand accounts read like an episode of *Mission Impossible*.

In late October 1943 the Front de l'Independence—an anti-Nazi coalition of political parties, labor, youth partisans, Catholic youth, Jewish resistance, and the clandestine press—was searching for an idea for a dramatic Armistice Day action when one of their leaders, Marc Aubrion, came up with the highly implausible idea of a mock edition of *Le Soir* to be distributed through the regular newspaper outlets. The dazzling audacity of the scheme tickled their Belgian sense of humor, but it was an awesome undertaking. In only eighteen days they had to locate a large printing press, procure sufficient newsprint, recruit editors and writers and cartoonists, find carriers and vehicles—and raise money, lots of money.

Madame Andrée Grandjean, lawyer at the Court of Appeals, raised 50,000 francs in two days. Ferdinand Wellens, owner of a large press, agreed to do the printing. Théo Mullier, a *Le Soir* employee and director of the illegal Front de l'Independence cell at the plant, arranged to steal the "flan," or mold of the masthead, and to provide the lists of kiosks and other distribution points. Three editors were recruited from the pool of the underground press (three hundred illegal newspapers were published in Belgium during the occupation!) to produce the edition.

Timing was the crucial element. The mock edition had to reach the newsstands just minutes before the paper's usual delivery time. To make sure this would happen, the conspirators planned actions to delay the distribution of the regular *Le Soir*. They considered three options; (1) sabotaging the presses; (2) setting fire to the delivery trucks as they were getting ready to leave the plant; and (3) arranging for an RAF air raid for the afternoon of the event (from Mullier they had learned that midday air alerts delayed delivery of the newspaper.) The first option was discarded as too dangerous for their own people in the plant. But the second was to be carried out by the youth partisans, who planned to create a diversion and then set fire to the trucks. And through the secret wireless to London they got a commitment for the third option: an RAF raid on Brussels.

Things did not go as planned, however. The youth partisans were not able to pull off the action at the trucks, and though two RAF planes did fly over Brussels at 2:00 P.M., they were a day late! So *Le Soir Volé* (*The Stolen le Soir*) reached the kiosks on schedule—but *Le Faux Soir* (*The False Le Soir*), as the Belgians lovingly and pridefully named it, had triumphantly arrived fifteen minutes earlier.

Five thousand copies were sold through the kiosks and book shops in Brussels before the Gestapo got wind of the hoax, and 45,000 more were sold in Brussels and the surrounding cities through the network of the Front de l'Independence. Copies later sold on the black market for as high as 2,000 francs. All of Belgium laughed at the humiliation of the Germans. Of the many exploits of the resistance, *Le Faux Soir* was among its proudest.

Like every act of the resistance, this one was not achieved without its martyrs. Ferdinand Wellens, the printer, and Théo Mullier, the *Le Soir* employee, were caught and tortured by the

Gestapo; they died in prison. Julien Oorlynk, a linotypist, and Henri Vanderveld, a printer, were also arrested and sent to a concentration camp in Czechoslovakia.

As I said of the Thibauts earlier, all these people had consciously joined a movement, committed themselves to fight to the end, and knew the consequences of their commitment.

It is much too early to forget.

Epilogue. Debriefing

Lexington, Kentucky, October 1988.

"The purpose of this roundtable is unfinished business. When we returned from missions like Münster and Schweinfurt, we were debriefed completely and in depth. Of course we got a tumbler of bourbon to loosen us up a little so we could talk about everything that happened on the plane—malfunctions, flak spottings, planes shot down, the number of parachutes that came out. But on our last mission we were not debriefed. In fact we were spread to the winds."

Dr. C. Leland Smith's southern drawl was more pronounced than I remembered from forty-five years earlier, when Smitty was the sensitive, inquisitive navigator on our crew. Now a professor of education at the University of Kentucky, he had organized this reunion with the same attention to detail that he had practiced when preparing his maps for a mission. He invited the Bramwell crew and their wives down to his and Sarah's farm near Lexington, Kentucky, and—having a sense of drama—arranged for our "debriefing" to be videotaped before an audience at the university's College of Education for TV news coverage and a follow-up story in the *Lexington Herald-Leader*.

Seated at the table were six surviving members of the crew—pilot Bill Bramwell, copilot Jim Current, bombardier John Maiorca, navigator Smitty Smith, assistant radio operator Leslie Meader, and assistant flight engineer George Watt. Tail gunner John Craig and radio operator Albertus Harrenstein, killed in combat, had gone down with our ship. Flight engineer H.C.

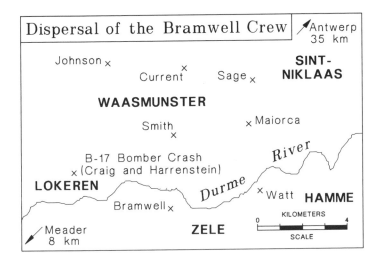

Johnson had died in 1968, and ball turret gunner Joseph Sage died in 1985.

Sharing in the warmth of the reunion were Virginia Bramwell, Sarah Smith, Eileen Meader, Marilyn Current, and Margie Watt. Betty Maiorca, unfortunately, was unable to attend. Five of the couples were already married when we went overseas in 1943, and we felt we had beaten the odds. The women too were veterans of the war.

Now, for the first time, six of us were able to tell each other what had happened in the last three or four minutes before the plane crashed.

William Bramwell had wavy white hair and distinguished looks but was still the same modest, self-effacing guy I remember. When the P-47's left us, he recalled, he still felt we were going to make it. Off to his right was Antwerp, and he could clearly see the English Channel up ahead. Home looked tantalizingly within reach.

Then everything happened at once: the ear-shattering thunderclap of an exploding 20mm shell in the cockpit, fire, acrid smoke, hydraulic fluid oozing all over, hot metal piercing his right side, and the ship plummeting toward the ground. His body was racked with pain, and he was losing blood, but he thought of only one thing: he had to gain control. While I was helplessly pinned in the waist, reviewing my life in anticipation of the inevitable crash, he and Current were busy fighting the control column with everything they had. The plane dropped some 12,000 feet before they could pull it out of its dive.

The phones were dead, so Bramwell sent Current to the nose and Johnson to the rear to see that the men got out. "I set the trim tab all the way back. I stood up between the two seats and held the plane level until I thought the crew in the front was able to get out. Then I dropped down through the hatch and lo and behold, there was Jim lit right on his back. Smitty and John were battling the hatch in the nose trying to get it open. As I recall, I indicated to Jim to go up to the bomb bay. I reached in under the pilot seat and pulled the emergency release for the bomb bay doors.

"I don't remember bailing out of the airplane. My next memory is hanging in the chute and my oxygen mask flopping around. I pulled it loose and tossed it away. And it just stayed there!"

"I looked up to see about a third of the shroud lines cut, with one line in the center. The chute opened, and I began to oscillate back and forth. As the swing went into the open side, the air dumped and I fell straight down again. As soon as I started falling straight down, it would open up. The next thing I knew, I was lying on the ground, and there were some people around."

Bramwell did not remember falling on telephone lines as reported by eyewitnesses many years later. He hit the ground hard, suffering a severe compression of the spine in addition to the twenty-seven shrapnel wounds along his right side. Villagers carried him to a nearby house and called a local doctor, but the

Germans arrived and threw him "like a sack of potatoes" into the rear of a small car.

He was taken to the basement of German headquarters near Ghent, where Smith, Current, Meader, and Sage were already prisoners. Meader recalls that in spite of his wounds, the first thing Bramwell said was, "I should have taken evasive action."

Bramwell landed in a prison hospital, spent eight months in a body cast, and was eventually transferred to a POW camp in Sagan where the "Great Escape" had occurred. Sent home in a prisoner exchange in February 1945, he was given a disability retirement, never to pilot a plane again.

Hearing his story for the first time was a deeply moving experience. I had had no inkling how badly wounded he had been and how much he had suffered all these years.

William (Jim) Current, now living in Atlanta, had retired with the rank of colonel after twenty-three years in the air force and spent an additional twenty-one years as a safety engineer for Lockheed. But when he started to talk, I saw that tow-headed nineteen-year-old kid again with that same enthusiasm and humor and competence.

Jim remembered how dangerous the mission was from the start: "We took off in a blinding fog and had to climb straight ahead for five minutes, turn 90 degrees for five minutes, then 90 degrees again. We had to climb for two or three hours before we got to altitude. Unfortunately, there were other aircraft all around doing the same thing. We were fortunate that we weren't killed a dozen times. Knowing these things there was a certain—what we used to call a 'pucker factor,' because you'd sit there all puckered up till you got through to the top.

"After that shell hit the cockpit, both of us were hanging on the wheel, holding it back and trying to keep the thing going. Poor Bill, he'd just been plastered from one end to the other with flak and injured very seriously. Then he motioned me toward the nose. I got down to the hatch. Smitty had been knocked out from lack of oxygen; John had just brought him to. We're banging away on the door. I bang on it till my hands are bloody. I couldn't get the door open. Then I realized—it was brought back to me rather forcibly by the navigator!—I was lying on top of the navigator while I was banging on the door!

"In the meantime this airplane is in a steep dive, but it turns, and as you look over your shoulder, here's the ground coming at you very rapidly. I went up through the bomb bay and briefly saw one of the gunners, and he said, 'Okay, we're clear.' And the next thing I remember is slamming against the bomb bay door. My arm ached about six months from hitting it. I tumble, I yank the rip cord real fast because I expect to go splat on the ground any minute. I open. I swing a couple of times and boomp, I land in the middle of a big plowed field, crunch like this, and see all these guys with all these nasty little guns, machine guns, coming at me. So I reach in and take my .45 and I say, 'Look fellahs' and I throw it away, like that. They come up and haul me away."

Current inexplicably was taken to Fort Breendonk—the concentration camp where Henri Malfait was sent two months later—but wound up at Stalag Luft I, the officers' camp located in Barth on the Baltic Sea, where he and Smitty spent the rest of the European war until they were liberated by the Russians.

John Maiorca told his story with cool deliberation, at times waxing poetic. "We hadn't quite reached the IP where we start on our bomb run when the plane was hit the first time. We must have risen forty feet. Then I heard, "Fire!"—the most dreaded thing a flyer can expect. We swung off. I flipped the bomb bay doors open and dropped the bombs—that lethal load we didn't need. We were over Germany, and we had clearance to drop our bombs anywhere in Germany. Smitty and I are pinned up against the roof. All our ammunition is with us. All the maps, all our equipment is up there with us. We just hung there. When we leveled off, of course, we both came down, and everything came down with us.

"Somebody made a call to check stations. We got no response from the tail gunner and no response from the navigator. I turned around and here Smitty is, stretched out. I grabbed an emergency canister and plunked it on to his face. He's coming slowly to, and he's getting a little belligerant, because this is the effect you get from lack of oxygen. When he came to, we got a heading and we started for home, but soon after the fighter escort left, we came under attack. Finally one of the shells exploded in the pilot's compartment, wounded Smitty and wounded me. Smitty reached down and tried to open the escape hatch in the nose. He couldn't get it open, so he started up to the pilot's compartment, and I was following him; I don't think you could have put a piece of paper between the two of us. He turned his head and said, 'It's time to go.' I immediately spun around, went back to the escape hatch. As I pulled the handle, I kicked the hatch. Out went the door. I crouched down, watched the ground go by, and out I went.

"I decided I'm going to free-fall for a while just to see what the situation is like. I reach for my rip cord. It's not there. So here I am, grabbing for everything I can find. This thing had slipped out of its pocket, was over my left shoulder. As I put my hand up. I could feel the cable. So I grabbed it.

"When I landed, I hid my chute and life jacket and started to run. Then I realized my high-altitude boots were impeding my running. So I stopped beside a small body of water, took the boots off, and threw them in. They flew through the air and landed right on their soles. They didn't sink! I picked up a limb and retrieved them, filled them with water, and they sank. I started to run again. I looked up and saw the other chutes still coming down, some distance away. I stopped at a barn behind a house and sat there taking stock. Here I am in the middle of Belgium somewhere. I've got a wife and a son back in the U.S.

They're going to be shocked in the next day or so. I'm going to have to make the best of it.

"Just about that time I heard a knock on the barn. The window opens and a lady looks out. C'mon in. So I walked around the barn, went into the house. She offered me coffee and some bread, which I declined. She told me to go into the barn, where she hid me under a pile of grain. I soon fell asleep."

That night a man and woman came for Maiorca with three bikes, and they rode in the dark to the man's house. The man offered to take John to the French border, but when John learned that the Belgian faced death if caught with an American flyer, he declined the offer. Early the next morning, now wearing civilian clothes, he set out on foot toward France. He walked twenty-seven miles in a cold rain—the same cold rain that Dr. Proost had braved in Brussels, looking for help for me. By a stroke of good fortune, John found someone who took him in. Later, resistance leaders Marcel Windels, Joseph Duthoy, and Leon Duyck, Waregem police chief, connected him with the Comet Line.

"I fell into all kinds of situations that make this, in the recounting, seem like a lark. People there had very little food to share with downed flyers, and here I fall in with the chief of the black market. His nickname was Al Capone. So I'm coming up with steaks, mushrooms, soups, the best of everything. I wind up in Paris, and the people I'm staying with ask me where would I like to go. So I pick Sacre Coeur, Napoleon's Tomb, the Eiffel Tower. Each and every day that I'm there, the man takes me out sightseeing. The Germans are all over. He says, 'Just act natural. Keep your mouth shut. Your identification papers say you're a deaf mute, so don't make a sound.'"

Thereafter, with the help of the Line, Maiorca made it to Spain, to Gibraltar, and back to England, where H.C. Johnson and I ran into him again in January 1944.

Smitty told his story in slow, measured tones, controlling his

strong emotions. "I was with Maiorca in the nose. And it is clear
that the oxygen system was damaged. I must have almost passed
out, and this character I'm sure saved my life. He pinned an
oxygen bottle on me, and I got belligerent. I told him to get his
damned hands off my face. He said, 'All right, Smitty. Die! See
if I care.' Within a few seconds I was with it. With anoxia you
become euphoric. It's like a high. And I was feeling, we're going
to make it. I was poring over the maps in front of me, and Bill
was asking for a heading back, and I concluded that a crippled
plane ditching in the North Sea is not much to look forward to.
So I gave him a heading around 270, hoping to hit Calais and a
short distance then across to the banks of Great Britain.

"When we were jumped by the Focke-Wulf, John and I
immediately got our guns ready for them to pass by. Which I
recall now was a stupid thought because no Focke-Wulf would
pass by the nose. He'd stand back there out of range and lob
those 20mm's into us. Then the shell exploded in the pilot's
compartment up over my head, and the shock was worse than the
wound. Because it lifted me up and all the radar equipment went
up with me. At that moment—at least, that is my recollection—
the nose went straight up. Nothing but blue skies. I said, 'Oh.
We are in bad trouble. We are in bad trouble.' Then the plane
goes into a terrifying dive. I was on the floor, swirling around,
the maps, gun cases, everything. I could smell the smoke
coming into the nose, and I thought we were going to hit any
moment.

"Finally and miraculously the plane leveled out. That was of
course Bill's last attention to it. I crawled through the bulkhead
between the nose and the pilot compartment where the escape
hatch was, and pulled the handle completely out. Nothing
happened. Current had fallen on top of me, and I could see his
boot coming down by my face, jumping up and down on the
escape hatch. And he couldn't get it open. Current left, and I
went up through the pilot compartment. The plane was flying

itself. Like a ghost ship. I'm terrified. I went through the top turret—taking a piece of my elbow, knee, head—to the bomb bay. At the other end of the bomb bay stood H.C. Johnson, just outside the radio shack. He looked at me and I looked at him and dived out the bomb bay.

"I landed in a field near the Waasmunster Ruiterskerk church, twenty feet from a fifteen-year-old boy, which terrified him as much as it terrified me. I tried to hide my chute. I went to a house for some water. I tried to trade for civilian clothes, and then suddenly the Germans were on me."

Smitty landed in hospitals in Ghent and Brussels before being transferred to Stalag Luft I for the duration.

Meader, as midwestern as they come, with a wry sense of humor, spoke quietly. "All I remember is that F-W 190 bearing at us. I tried to fire at him, but he was behind the tail and I couldn't get him. All of a sudden something hot hit my back. I feel a burn on the neck and the back, and then the plane goes into this big dive. Now you have to understand this is an open waist. The noise is just tremendous. You've never heard such a racket in your life, with the air rushing through. The plane is diving, the parachutes are up on the ceiling. We're diving. I'm scared. But then the plane leveled off, the parachutes came down, and George and I tried to get that door open and couldn't. He lunged at it, and away he went. Being a gentleman from Minnesota, I held the door open for Joe Sage—'After you, Joe'—and he went out. And then I tried to squeeze through that door, and lo and behold, I was dangling in the air! My parachute harness was caught on the door. People asked me later if that was when my hair turned white. It seemed like an eternity—but it was only a few seconds. I pulled myself up the straps, grabbed hold of the door, let go of the straps, and fell.

"Not knowing our altitude, I pulled the rip cord right away because the plane had dived quite a bit. And the peace, the quiet.

You could see the German plane. You could see our plane. The sun was shining. No wind. I landed in a plowed field right by a road near a farmhouse. And I didn't even drag like you see in the movies. I did a deep knee bend and stood up. But on the way down I had seen German soldiers coming on their bicycles. They called a doctor, patched me up, and I was a prisoner. So that's short and simple."

Actually it wasn't quite that short and simple. He had a nasty wound; Smitty describes seeing Meader all "stapled up" around the neck. He was sent to a prison hospital in Brussels and then spent a year and a half together with Joe Sage in the notorious Stalag XVII B in Krems, Austria. "It wasn't anything like the movie or the TV series," Meader told me.

When we'd all related our stories, the last bit of unfinished business—Smitty called it an "autopsy"—was to determine the distribution of the landings of the men and the final course of our ship. Smitty had not lost his navigator's touch. Projecting a map onto a large screen, he pinpointed the exact touchdown of each crew member and the site of our plane crash. We noted the order and perceived altitude when each one jumped, when the chutes were opened, and the landing locations. We followed the flight of the plane as it reversed direction and plunged into the cemetery at Lokeren.

"The *Forteresse* wanted to return to Germany," one of the Waasmunster eyewitnesses had said.

The last mission of the Bramwell crew was now debriefed.

Index